the jewish princess cookbook

having your cake & eating it...

Georgie Tarn & Tracey Fine

McBooks Press, Inc.
ithaca, ny

www.mcbooks.com

The Jewish Princess Cookbook
having your cake & eating it
Georgie Tarn & Tracey Fine

McBooks Press, Inc.
www.mcbooks.com
Ithaca, New York

Published by McBooks Press 2008
First published in 2006 by
Quadrille Publishing Ltd., London

Text © 2006
Georgie Tarn & Tracey Fine
Illustrations C 2006 Karen Greenberg
Design and layout C 2006 Quadrille
Publishing Limited

ISBN: 978-1-59013-161-9

Library of Congress Cataloging-in-Publication Data
Tarn, Georgie.
   The Jewish princess cookbook : having your
cake & eating it / Georgie Tarn & Tracey Fine.
      p. cm.
   Includes index.
   ISBN 978-1-59013-161-9 (cloth : alk. paper)
   1. Jewish cookery. 2. Jewish women-Humor. I.
Fine, Tracey. II. Title.
   TX724.T346 2008
   641.5'676-dc22

2007041231

Additional copies of this book may be ordered
from any bookstore or directly from McBooks Press,
Inc., ID Booth Building, 520 North Meadow St.,
Ithaca, NY 14850. Please include $5.00 postage
and handling with mail orders. Shipping within the
U.S. is free for multiple book orders over $75.00.
New York State residents must add sales tax to
total remittance (books & shipping). All McBooks
Press publications can also be ordered by calling
toll-free 1-888-BOOKS11 (1-888-266-5711).

Please call to request a free catalog.
Visit the McBooks Press website at
www.mcbooks.com.

Printed and bound in Singapore

9 8 7 6 5 4 3 2 1

dedication

This book is dedicated to our grandmothers, who are truly loved and missed. They always had the luxury of time when it came to their grandchildren. They inspired us to cook delicious food. They never worried about their waistlines (this made us worry about ours). They always had an opinion on everything: even if they were wrong, they were right. They handed down to us a wonderful sense of *Yiddishkeit*. They gave us heartfelt cuddles within their enormous, non-surgically enhanced breasts. They made our families' lives more colorful with their ability to start *broygeses*.

To Grandma Kitty and Nana Lily.
We are sure you are *schlepping naches*
from up above!

contents

acknowledgments

As I'll explain in a minute, this book grew out of a midlife crisis. I have to say that Tracey and I found this crisis great fun, complete with loads of hysterical telephone conversations and jumping up and down outside very swanky offices in London's West End (certainly recapturing our youth—circa age 11). Through all the excitement I actually lost loads of weight without even having to sniff the gym—fantastic! So as I sit here thinking about my midlife crisis, my advice would be that if you are contemplating one of your own, and you are a Jewish Princess, just make sure it's one that is PPP: Positive, Productive, and of course, Princess-like.

Now, on to the business at hand, which is thanking people.

We are surrounded by incredible friends. I say "incredible" not only because they seem to know everyone in the world, but also because of how unselfish and generous they have all been with their advice. It really has been a revelation that all my friends' husbands and boyfriends are actually incredibly knowledgeable, professional, and *smart*, because when we go out and about, visit the latest restaurants, etc., etc., you only think of them as *Husbands* or *Boyfriends* (need I say more?). You never think of them as directing boardroom meetings or taking on their own global, midlife crises. They are just people you love and adore, make fun of (in an affectionate way, of course!), and have a great time with.

We would like to thank our mothers, Sandra Chester and Helen Fine (yes, now you can tell your friends); our fathers, David Chester and Tony Fine, who always answer emergency JP phone calls, even on the golf course; and in-laws Bobbie and Irvin Tarn, whose bathroom stop proved invaluable on the way up to those West End meetings. We would, of course, like to thank Georgie's husband, RAT, and Tracey's partner, Richard de Smith, who have been our "rocks"; our children—Cassie, Eden, Darcy, Max, and Channie—whose talents have contributed to this work; and our brothers and sisters, nieces and nephews who have enjoyed sampling The Ultimate Friday Night Dinners again and again and again.

Then there's Anne Marie Owens (The Hairdresser), who knew Dorie Simmonds (The Agent), who knew Quadrille (The Publisher), where we met the wonderful Jane O'Shea. Thanks, too, to Stephen Marks, for all the phone calls regarding net and gross—yes, we've finally got it ("gross you get, net you vet"); Paul Taylor, for slotting us in between his high-powered business meetings; Roger Law, for meeting us for a cup of tea, a slice of cake, and inspirational advice; William Miller, for your time and patience; and Ray Simone, for believing in us.

And thank you Mel Goldberg (you were there from the start); Andrew Thompson, our lawyer (who had no idea what he was getting into); and Debbie Jones, our bank manager (we love you—you gave us a credit card!). We would like to thank our most understanding editor, Jamie Ambrose, who has been in intensive JP training; designer Claire Peters; PR (Princess Relations) people Clare Lattin and Emily Sanders; and all at Quadrille for making our Princess wish come true.

Finally, big thanks to the Jewish Princesses: Karen Gerrard, Elaine Grant, Zilda Collins, Lisa Marks, Sima Fine, Deborah Bright, Mandy Stanley, Auntie Rosalind Chester, Sharon Payne, Michelle Grossman, and Sylvia de Smith for parting with their precious family recipes, and last but not least, Andrea (Princess G's *au pair*).

1

introduction

princess philosophy

I'm proud to admit that I am a Jewish Princess. I believe that every woman has a little bit of a JP in her—or if she doesn't, then she certainly should.

So just what *is* a Jewish Princess, I hear you ask? Well, the usual stereotype seems to be "spoiled little rich girl who spends all her days shopping and beautifying herself"—let me tell you, that is simply untrue and quite unfair. After all, I never spend *all* day shopping and beautifying myself! I just like to enjoy life, and part of the enjoyment of life is food and feeding your family.

Do I love cooking? "Not particularly" is the answer to that, so why write a cookbook? Well, as I approached my fortieth birthday, I realized that I was having a midlife crisis—but of course, being a Jewish Princess, mine was taking a rather different turn. I wouldn't contemplate an affair, and I certainly wasn't going to have a nervous breakdown or cut off all my hair (heaven forbid!). No, my crisis was going to be *productive*, and as I seem to have inherited the good-cook gene from my mother (who now no longer cooks, but can be found somewhere in a Floridian mall) and my grandmother-over-shalom (a Jewish expression for when we speak of the passed-over—not Passover: that's a Jewish holiday), a cookbook seemed like the most natural thing to do. I mean, we all have to eat, and even Jewish Princesses can't go out to eat *every* night.

And if I have to do something, I like to do it well, even if it's not exactly at the top of my "Have to Do" list (which, by the way, is always *very* long).

So when the idea of *The Jewish Princess Cookbook* came to me, I immediately thought of my friends; after all, who else can you share all the memories with? I phoned my oldest and most Princess-like friend, Tracey, to ask her what she thought of the idea and whether she wanted to be involved. She considered it for about half a second and jumped aboard.

The first thing we did was to delegate our jobs on the book: I made lunch; she made the cake.

the power of food

Food and eating lie at the very center of Jewish culture. I really think the Old Testament was our first menu—the festivals give us such wonderful delicacies. When I think of Hanukkah, I think of doughnuts. The Jewish New Year? Honey cake. And so it goes on and on.

Just think of your favorite cake. Or, if you're not a "cake" person (*I* certainly don't know who you are, but maybe you're out there...) think of your favorite food. How does it make you feel?

When someone takes the time and trouble to make your favorite food, how do you feel about them?

Grateful. *Happy*.

Now, when people are grateful and *happy*, they are in your power. So forget the power of speech, the power of song, the power of the written word; let's get down to basics and realize that with a few eggs, some flour, and a good chunk of chocolate we have the power of making others *happy*. And happiness leads to a loving home, a loving partner—and of course, lovely *things*.

It really is true that the way to a Jewish man's heart is through his stomach. If you asked Jewish men whether they would prefer a nice bowl of chicken soup or a romp upstairs, I'll bet eight out of ten of them would go for the chicken soup—especially if it contained matzo balls.

Yet the Jewish Princess of today isn't like her mother or grandmother; she's not going to be a slave to the house or the kitchen. Today's Jewish Princess wants to run a wonderful home, look good, produce lovely food, look good, look after her children—did I mention "look good"? Sure, we want to have our cake and eat it, but we also want to look as if we *haven't*!

In order to do this, we have to have some tricks up our sleeves. While I have no objection to cheating in this area, and will admit sometimes to using convenience food and doctoring it to make it look like my own (oh, come *on*—we've all done it!), there truly is nothing like the satisfaction of producing wonderful homemade food.

Well, OK, there are many other satisfying things, such as 1) shopping, 2) shopping, and 3) shopping.

But I digress.

In order to have a very, very satisfying life, then, use *The Jewish Princess Cookbook* to produce food that is 1) easy, 2) non-time-consuming, and 3) has fewer than ten ingredients, on average, per recipe. Oh—and of course tastes delicious and looks incredibly difficult.

If *I* can do it, *you* can do it!

So take back your take-outs, stock up your pantries, plan ahead, try a little bit of imagination, and use this book. You will then have the power of food in your hands.

the pay-off

The power of food produces many valuable dividends. Respect and adoration are just two of these, and when you see your friends and family loving your food, it really does give you a feeling of immense satisfaction—especially when they think you've been slaving over a hot stove, and you haven't (but no need to correct them there).

The recipes you will find in *The Jewish Princess Cookbook* are simple, easy to follow, and have a fantastic success rate—but don't feel you have to be a slave to them. Whenever you cook, always think of the flavors you like and be creative. Use recipes, including the ones in this book, as guides, but if you want to add something or give the recipe a twist, try it. You never know what fantastic new thing you may discover.

Always remember: it's not only the food, but how you present it that earns the seal of approval from your friends and family. So go on: take the plunge. I'm sure you will still have time left over for all those other, more satisfying, and very important things.

Which reminds me...

Got to go now—hairdresser's appointment!

jewish dietary rules

Contrary to popular belief, the rules that govern the Jewish diet are *not:*

* EAT, EAT, EAT, or
* have a little (or a lot) of what you enjoy, or
* when you entertain, always make sure there is enough food
  in case your guests bring ten friends with them.

No, the Jewish dietary rules date back to the Old Testament (a best-seller.) In this book, the Jewish people were given strict rules that applied to every aspect of eating—partly because, you know, even in those days, Jewish Princesses were thinking about that four-letter word: *diet.*

If you thought the Atkins was tricky, or found the G.I. Diet a little difficult to follow, or decided that the Blood Type Diet was far too complicated (especially if you don't know your blood type), then let me put all this in perspective. These are nothing—NOTHING—compared to following the "K Diet," otherwise known as keeping kosher.

The Jewish kosher diet makes all others seem easy. It's complicated, you're on it for a lifetime, and sometimes it is very tempting to fall off the wagon. As far as the latter is concerned, it is up to every Jewish Princess to decide how disciplined she is prepared to be, but for anyone else who wants to try it, here are the highlights.

kosher meat

When it comes to meat, to follow the kosher diet you must only choose from animals that chew the cud and have split hooves—so beef and lamb are in and pork, camel, and horse are out. Which is fine by me; I personally would never dream of eating Black Beauty (or a camel).

Not only are certain animals forbidden, but certain cuts of meat must also be avoided. However, if you buy your meat from a kosher butcher, you will never go wrong, as I can assure you they are very strict about the kinds and cuts of meat that are stocked on their shelves.

Fish are a little more straightforward. You can eat all fish which have scales and fins, but all types of shellfish are not permitted.

treif and parev

All unkosher food is known as *treif,* which actually means "torn." This does not mean torn between choosing Parma ham or just having the melon; it means you're not allowed to eat flesh that has been torn from one animal by another animal. All animals killed in this manner are forbidden.

Also, milk and meat must not be eaten together at the same meal, so no hamburgers—or should I say "beefburgers"?—with milk shakes.

Foods that contain neither milk nor meat are known as *parev.* This means these foods can be eaten with either meat or dairy meals: for example, fish, fruit, vegetables, and non-animal, manufactured food products such as non-dairy creamers.

If this all sounds like a lot of palaver, there is a bright side. For every Jewish Princess, keeping a kosher home means the added bonus of being able to indulge in buying not one, but at least *two* sets of dishes, cutlery, saucepans, and linen in order to keep all those milky and meaty dishes separate. Of course, you should never need an excuse to hit the housewares department of your favorite store, but this at least validates the urge.

As you can see, the basis of a kosher diet is something that requires discipline and willpower. Luckily for you, I've already done the hard work of making sure that all the recipes in this book are kosher.

For all Jewish Princesses who make the decision to follow this way of eating, I just want to say:

Mazel tov! You're following the oldest diet in the book.

What does a Jewish Princess
make for dinner?

Reservations!

a word about life

Now before you start trying the recipes, I want to share with you a very important part of JP philosophy. You might not catch on immediately, but bear with me, please, and read on to the end. There's plenty of time for cooking afterward.

I love Champagne, especially Princess Pink Champagne (naturally). I love the bottle: curvaceous and crowned with gold. A dry *pop!* The cork is released, and there's the slow descent of the liquid into a tall, slim glass. The color is unique: like liquid candlelight. This perfect drink is to be sipped and savored, and it reminds me of all the good times in my life.

Except, actually, the first time I ever drank it.

I was 16 years old, out on a date, and dressed to kill in a new lilac leather dress (well, it *was* the early '80s). I wanted to impress this boy-man sitting in front of me, and being a very sophisticated teenage Princess, I ordered a Champagne cocktail. Unfortunately, nerves and an empty stomach got the better of me, and I spent most of the evening in the ladies' room, trying to dry my leather belt which accidentally got flushed down the toilet. This unfortunate incident did not cool my ardor for Champagne, however. I just left out the cocktail part after that and went for the pink stuff straight.

And here's where the philosophy bit comes in. You see, above all else, the Jewish Princess knows that life is for living—that's with a capital "L." This isn't a dress rehearsal, after all (though dresses do, of course, play a very important part in every Jewish Princess's life).

The first rule of being a JP is this: if there is an excuse to celebrate—like buying your first pair of Jimmy Choos, or even when (not if) the first recipe you try in this book is a success—then bring on and bring out the Champagne. This cool, delicious beverage makes every occasion a celebration.

You could try it right now, just to get the hang of it. Fill your glass and toast: to life—*lechayim!*

the princess pledge

* I pledge to have a clean and tidy home (but I never said I would do the cleaning and tidying).

* I pledge to acknowledge and embrace my *mishegasses*, because they make me who I am.

* I pledge that I will be prepared to go on vacation, even at very, very short notice.

* I pledge to buy lots of evening shoes and make sure I wear them.

* I pledge to have the bling, but not to wear everything (at once).

* I pledge that if I find an item of clothing that's really me, I will buy it in more than one color.

* I pledge to give rather than receive (except when it comes to jewelry).

* I pledge that I will make the most of myself, embrace the good parts, and visit the plastic surgeon for the bad parts.

* I pledge that when I visit public restrooms, I will do the "Princess Perch."

* I pledge that I will respect my manicurist, hairdresser, and beautician, for they are in the background, allowing me to step into the foreground.

* I pledge to treasure my true friends, because they are the diamonds that every girl needs.

* I swear allegience to Gucci, Louis Vuitton, Prada, D&G, Dior, Missoni, DKNY, Chanel, Yves Saint Laurent, Fendi, Mui Mui, Mark Jacobs, Tod's, Jimmy Choo, Etro, Moschino, Calvin Klein, Hermès, Lanvin, Givenchy, Thierry Mugler, Roberto Cavalli, Marni, Georgio Armani, La Perla, Juicy Couture, Seven Jeans, Citizens of Humanity, Escada, Bottega Veneta, Alexander McQueen, Versace, Vivien Westwood, Diane von Furstenberg, Stella McCartney, Burberry, Emanuel Ungaro, Ralph Lauren, Chloé, Valentino, Graff, Cartier, Kauffman de Suisse, Tiffany, Asprey, Rolex, Chopard, Van Cleef & Arples, David Morris, Boodles, and Bvlgari. I apologize to any I've missed, but I'm sure I'll be visiting your store soon!

2

appetizers

appetizer surprisers

I really look forward to visiting a new, stylish, "spendy" type of restaurant. All too often, however, we end up at a "once-r": the restaurant you visit only once because the service and food are so bad and the prices so high that you'd never dream of going back for seconds. It generally happens this way:

As I take in the beautiful surroundings, I hope the menu will arrive promptly so I can savor my glass of the pink stuff. Eventually the waiter notices me (the one at the center table, gesticulating wildly) and we order—well, *I* order, as Hubby seems to think I'll somehow magically know what he wants. At this point I have to resort to sign language, either because the waiter doesn't speak a word of English, or because the restaurant is so noisy (due to designer stone floors, stainless-steel walls, and chattering people) that normal speech is impossible.

Then The Wait begins—and so does my sense of Food Foreboding. I've ordered a *hot* appetizer, and seeing that the encounter with the waiter hasn't gone well, I'll be surprised if it's not lukewarm when my fork makes contact.

What is it with once-r restaurants? They charge a fortune, yet make you wait an eternity before delivering anything. By the time the appetizer appears, you've already eaten a loaf of bread, a bowl of olives, and nuts from the bar. Now, I usually find the appetizer the most enjoyable part of the meal. Why? Well, by the time I've finished the breadbasket, the olives and nuts, had words with the manager, and munched my way through the first course, I'm simply too full and too exhausted to enjoy anything else.

After many such disastrous dinners I now really look forward to being entertained by friends, or to entertaining them in my own home. Even though my abode may be a little last season, the chairs are comfortable, the pink stuff is ready and waiting, and the food always arrives on time. I also know that when I serve appetizers (at the *correct* temperature), my guests will enjoy them, but they'll still have plenty of appetite left to relish the rest of their meal—and I *know* they'll be coming back for seconds!

pink grapefruit with brown sugar

serves *as many as you like!*

pink grapefruit
  (allow 1 per person)

dark brown sugar
  (2 teaspoons per person)

Peel the pink grapefruit, removing all of the seeds and as much pith as possible.

Cut each into segments.

Place the segmented grapefruit into a frying pan and sprinkle with the sugar.

Cook briefly over a high heat—as the sugar melts, toss the grapefruit segments so that the fruit is well-coated. This whole process takes less than two minutes, so you could say it'll be ready in a jiffy.

Serve in individual glass dishes.

This is a delicious, easy appetizer, warm and sweet on the outside and cool and zingy on the inside.

melon balls in champagne

serves 6

1 cantaloupe
1 honeydew melon
about ¾ cup champagne, or other
   white sparkling wine

4 tablespoons clear honey
whites of 2 medium eggs, beaten
¾ cup superfine sugar

Ball both melons and mix the pieces in a bowl.

Mix the Champagne and honey, then pour over the melon balls.

Chill.

Take some Champagne glasses and dip the rim of each into the beaten egg white, then into the sugar.

Spoon the melon mixture into the glasses, making sure there is plenty of liquid in each glass.

Lechayim!

watermelon with feta cheese

serves *as many as you like!*

1 watermelon (preferably
   seedless)—allow five small
   pieces per person
vodka
feta cheese, cubed—allow
   ten cubes per person

virgin olive oil
1 basil leaf per person,
   for decoration

Cut the watermelon into slices and remove the rind (and seeds, if there are any). Place the slices in the shape of a flower on each plate.

Drizzle a little vodka over the melon.

Place ten small cubes of feta cheese around the edge of each plate.

Drizzle a small amount of olive oil over the cheese.

Place a basil leaf in the middle of each plate for decoration.

A delicious, refreshing, quick-and-simple appetizer that looks wonderful. Jewish Princesses will love it!

chopped herring

serves 8

1 lb sweet herring fillets,
  with onion
2 eating apples, peeled
  and grated
2 medium hard-boiled eggs

6 graham crackers
1 tablespoon ground almonds
1 slice of white bread,
  crusts removed
2 teaspoons sugar

Drain the herrings and pat dry with a paper towel.

Mix all of the ingredients in a food processor until smooth.

This is delicious served with toasted black bread and cream cheese.

easy salmon pâté

serves 6 as an appetizer, 4 for a girly lunch

1 skinless salmon fillet
(approximately 9 oz)
1 skinless rainbow trout fillet
(approximately 9 oz)
1 bunch of fresh dill
1 medium onion, peeled
2 lemons

salt and black pepper to taste
5 teaspoons creamed horseradish
1 heaping tablespoon sour cream
3 tablespoons low-fat
natural yogurt
6 oz unsliced smoked salmon

Wash and place the salmon and rainbow trout in a saucepan
along with half the dill, the onion, and the juice of one of
the lemons. Season with salt and black pepper, then cover
with water.

Bring the fish to a boil and boil for one minute.

Turn off the heat (if you're using an electric stove, move the fish away)
and cover. The fish will continue on cooking in the hot water.

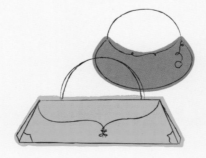

After 30 minutes, remove the fish from the saucepan and place in a bowl.

In a separate bowl, mix the horseradish, sour cream, yogurt, and the juice of half a lemon.

Add the rest of the dill, finely chopped (I use kitchen scissors), and some salt and pepper to season.

When the fish has cooled, add the creamed horseradish mixture and blend well until the mixture forms a smooth pâté. Refrigerate.

Take a piece of aluminum foil or waxed paper and place the smoked salmon on top. Season with black pepper and lemon juice.

Spoon the fish pâté onto the smoked salmon, leaving a gap at the bottom so that you can easily roll the salmon lengthwise over the pâté.

Fold the smoked salmon over the pâté, making a parcel in the shape of a tube.

Wrap the foil or waxed paper over the salmon, then refrigerate.

Before serving, remove the foil or paper and cut into slices. You can decorate it with thin slices of lemon, if desired.

This appetizer looks very impressive indeed—so give yourself a pâté on the back!

caramelized onion, tomato, and brie tart

serves 6

6 onions, peeled and thinly sliced
2 tablespoons of olive oil
3 tablespoons sugar
1 lb ready-to-roll
  frozen puff pastry
a sprinkling of all-purpose flour

about 25 firm cherry tomatoes
9 oz mild, creamy brie
dash of olive oil
salt and pepper to taste
fresh basil leaves (enough to
  scatter over the dish)

Preheat the oven to 350°F.

In a large pan, fry the onion slices in the 2 tablespoons olive oil until softened. Add the sugar and continue frying, stirring constantly, until they turn a deep golden brown.

Roll out the pastry so that it is just large enough to fit an 11-inch pie plate or tart pan. Line the pan with the pastry.

Sprinkle some all-purpose flour lightly over the surface of the pastry, then spread a thin layer of caramelized onion on top of the flour.

Halve the tomatoes and lay them around the pastry in rings, slightly overlapping, until you get to the center. Cover all areas quite tightly, since the tomatoes will shrink when cooked.

Slice the brie thinly and place the slices on top of the tomatoes, leaving a 1-inch gap between pieces, since it will melt and spread.

Sprinkle with a dash of olive oil, then add the salt, pepper, and basil.

Bake in the preheated oven for 35 minutes. The pastry should be golden brown. Serve warm or cold.

This simple dish looks spectacular. It's lovely for lunch.

The first Jewish Princess, Eve,
decided that her partner needed
to be put on a healthier regime.
So for starters he would have
to eat a piece of fruit a day.

Unfortunately, she chose the
wrong one.

roasted asparagus with lemon mayo

serves 4

2 tablespoons low-fat mayonnaise
2 tablespoons sour cream
juice of 1 lemon
  (divided into two portions)

sea salt and black pepper
2 large bunches of asparagus
extra virgin olive oil

First, make the lemon mayonnaise. Combine the mayonnaise, sour cream, and half the lemon juice. Season with sea salt and black pepper to taste. Refrigerate.

Preheat the oven to 400°F.

Wash and trim the asparagus spears and place them in a nonstick roasting pan.

Drizzle them with the olive oil and the other half of the lemon juice. Turn the asparagus spears so that they have a fine coating of the olive oil and lemon juice on both sides.

Season with black pepper and sea salt to taste.

Roast the asparagus for 20 minutes, turning the spears halfway through cooking.

Take out of the oven and leave to cool. Once cold, refrigerate or serve immediately.

To serve, place the asparagus on a serving dish with the mayo on the side.

Delicious for dipping!

roasted red and yellow peppers

serves 6

7 red peppers
7 yellow peppers
1 cup canned pitted black
   olives, drained
1 tablespoon balsamic vinegar

olive oil to coat the peppers
   (infused with garlic or basil,
   if you prefer)
2 teaspoons sugar

Preheat the oven to 350°F.

Slice the peppers into large chunks and deseed.

Rinse the olives and add them to the peppers.

Place in an ovenproof dish and pour on a good splash
of balsamic vinegar.

Add enough olive oil so that the peppers are covered.

Sprinkle the sugar over the top.

Mix the ingredients together with a spatula.

Bake in the preheated oven for one hour, turning the peppers
every 20 minutes so they do not burn, until the vegetables are soft.

*This dish can be served by itself, or for an appetizer you can
make some toasted French bread pieces and put the peppers
on top, along with a handful of basil. For a main course, just
add a handful of cherry tomatoes to the above. It also makes
a delicious pasta sauce.*

salmon cakes

serves 6

12 oz canned red salmon
1 large onion, grated
1 large egg, beaten
salt and black pepper to taste

approximately ⅓ cup
    medium matzo meal
corn oil, for frying
sea salt, for serving

Combine the salmon, grated onion, and beaten egg. Add salt and pepper to taste, then add the matzo meal to bind the mixture.

Form the mixture into patties and fry in a wok or frying pan, using enough corn oil to cover. Fry until light brown.

Just before serving, grind a little sea salt over the fish cakes. They're extra-delicious if you serve them warm.

If you wish to give these a Thai-style twist, add some chopped cilantro and a little lemongrass paste. Use paper towels to rest the fried fish cakes on; this will remove any excess oil.

sesame chicken balls

serves 8 as an appetizer

1 lb ground chicken
4 teaspoons teriyaki marinade
3 tablespoons fine matzo meal
½ teaspoon sugar
2 medium eggs

half an onion, grated
salt and black pepper to taste
1½ cups sesame seeds
vegetable oil, for frying

Mix together all the ingredients except the sesame seeds. Season well with black pepper, adding a little salt to taste.

Wet your hands and roll the mixture into little balls, then dip each into a bowl filled with the sesame seeds, covering the chicken mixture.

Fry in vegetable oil until cooked.

Serve with dipping sauce on the side (you can use a sweet chili sauce or mango chutney), or serve with Chinese cabbage salad for a little bit of "Ko-chin"—Kosher Chinese!

spinach bake (kugel)

serves 6 as an appetizer, or 4 for lunchtime with the girls

¾ lb fine dry pasta
  (such as *lockshen* noodles)
¾ lb fresh spinach
2 tablespoons unsalted butter

1 pack onion soup mix
1½ cups mascarpone cheese
3 medium eggs
1 handful of pine nuts

Preheat the oven to 350°F.

Boil the pasta according to instructions on the packet until it's *al dente*.

Put the spinach in a saucepan with the butter and gently fry until limp.

Combine the soup mix with the cheese and eggs. Add the cooked pasta and spinach and mix well.

Grease an ovenproof pie dish and fill it with the mixture.

Sprinkle the pine nuts over the top.

Bake for an hour until crispy, or 15 minutes if cooking in individual greased ramekins.

Delicious served either hot or cold.

latkes (potato pancakes)

makes approximately 50 cocktail-sized pancakes

5 lb good-quality potatoes	salt and pepper to taste
3 large onions	3 large eggs
2 tablespoons self-rising flour	corn oil, for frying

Grate the potatoes and onions. Put them in a colander and press out all the liquid: place a sheet of paper towel on top, then place a heavy saucepan on top of the paper towel and leave for five minutes.

Put the potato-onion mixture into a bowl and add the flour, seasoning, and eggs.

Bind the mixture with the palms of your hands (take off all your jewelry first!). Take a spoonful of the mixture (about 2 teaspoons' worth), form it into a small, round ball and flatten it by pressing gently. At the same time, squeeze out any excess liquid.

Put a generous amount of oil in a large frying pan and heat.

Place the *latkes* in the pan and semi-deep-fry them. When one side is lightly brown, turn over and cook the other side.

Remove from the oil with a slotted spoon, drain, then place on paper towels to absorb the oil.

Eat immediately, or freeze. If frozen, place on a baking tray lined with parchment paper and heat in a moderate oven for 15 minutes.

Make these latkes *as small as you like for cocktail items, or medium-sized to serve with a main course. Delicious dipped in apple sauce.*

3

salads

salads your personal trainer would be proud of

I first discovered my love for salad as a child in the 1970s. Thinking back, my mother was a nutritional genius: she turned my brother and me on to raw vegetables with her unique "Clock Salad." This was a very '70s affair, straight out of *The Wonder Years*. It was a midweek supper which consisted of a large plate that had been sectioned with chopped vegetables, hard-boiled eggs, and even grated cheese, like a pizza. We were allowed to choose our own "sections." Because my mother got us involved and excited about which vegetables we could choose, my love for salad was born.

Of course, such things can be taken to extremes, particularly when you're least expecting it—or should I say when you're expecting? When I was pregnant with my third child, for example, I immediately had a strong craving for raw cucumber (thank G-d, not doughnuts).* I sniffed cucumber, munched whole cucumbers down in one bite, and even once had to leave a dinner party in search of a cucumber, smuggling it in and nibbling it out of my handbag!

Sometimes I still get a craving for salad and rush to my refrigerator to start chopping. Often, I'll use not only crispy, cold ingredients but I'll be inspired and add roasted vegetables, fruit, or even warm meat to make my own personal Princess salad.

Salads are colorful, crunchy, and for the Jewish Princess, guilt-free eating on a plate—well, they're guilt-free as long as you don't add too many fattening ingredients. When ordering a salad in a restaurant, for instance, I always ask for the dressing on the side; this saves on those unwanted calories. So go on: dive in!

*You may be wondering why this Princess writes G-d like this. I was always taught that you should never take G-d's name in vain, even when writing. If you don't spell it out, it doesn't count...

coleslaw

serves 6

1 white cabbage, shredded
2 large carrots, grated
5 tablespoons low-fat mayonnaise

1 tablespoon heavy cream
salt and black pepper to taste

Mix everything together thoroughly.

If you want "that something extra," add one handful of sliced almonds and one handful of raisins.

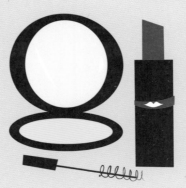

crunchy fruit and nut rice salad

serves 10

1 cup brown rice
1 cup white rice
1⅓ cups dried apricots
1 heaping cup dried figs
1 heaping cup sultanas
    (golden or white raisins)
salt and black pepper
½ cup pine nuts
½ cup mixed nuts
½ cup toasted sesame seeds

for the dressing
about ¼ cup white-wine vinegar
½ cup olive oil
2 teaspoons chopped fresh
    oregano (or 1 teaspoon dried)
2 teaspoons sugar

First, make the dressing by combining all the dressing ingredients.

Boil the brown and white rice separately and leave to cool.

Chop all the fruit into small pieces, mix well, then add the rice and season to taste.

Stir in the dressing.

Just before serving, add the pine nuts, mixed nuts, and sesame seeds and mix well.

Crunchy, colorful, and gives you loads of energy.

cucumber salad

serves 8

2 cucumbers
4 spring onions
4 tablespoons quark:
  a fresh white curd cheese
  from Germany (or other
  low-fat soft cheese)

1 bunch of chopped chives
6 mint leaves, chopped
salt and black pepper to taste

Wash and finely slice the cucumbers and spring onions.

Add the quark, chives, and mint leaves.

Mix well and season to taste.

This is a lovely, fresh-tasting salad.

green bean and tomato salad

serves 6

1 lb fresh green beans
½ lb small, tasty tomatoes
   (sweet cherry-type)
salt and black pepper to taste

approximately 3 tablespoons
   balsamic vinegar
1 handful fresh basil leaves

Wash and trim the beans. Place in a saucepan and cover with water.

Bring to a boil, then reduce the heat and simmer until the beans are cooked but still have a "bite" to them. Drain and place them in a bowl to cool.

Wash the tomatoes. Fill a heatproof bowl with boiling water. Place the tomatoes in the bowl and cover for five minutes.

Remove the tomatoes and peel them—the skin should come away easily.

Chop the tomatoes and add to the beans. Season to taste with salt and black pepper.

Add a good splash of balsamic vinegar—approximately three tablespoons.

Add the chopped basil.

Refrigerate until ready to serve.

This can be served as an accompaniment to a meat or fish dish, adding color and a crunch.

diamond carrot salad

serves 6–8

2¼ lb carrots, grated
1 large orange, sliced
2 tablespoons lemon juice
2 tablespoons sugar

1 cup fresh orange juice
¾ cup sultanas
   (white or golden raisins)

Mix together the first five ingredients, then add the raisins or sultanas.

This is even better if you let the raisins/sultanas soak overnight in the orange juice.

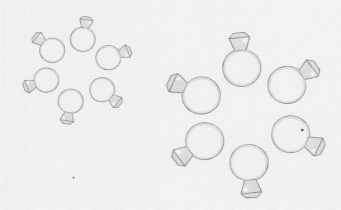

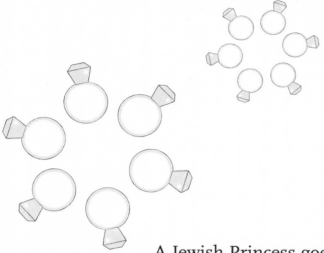

A Jewish Princess goes to visit her specialist.

She comes home and tells her husband she has been put on a very specific diet: she is only allowed karats—2.5 and over!

oriental cabbage salad

serves 8

1 white cabbage
1 orange, cut into small pieces
1 mango, chopped
2 handfuls of raisins
½ cup no-pulp orange juice

balsamic vinegar
olive oil
salt and black pepper
1 handful of sliced almonds

Dice the cabbage, orange, and mango and mix together.

Add the raisins.

Dress with the orange juice, a good splash of balsamic vinegar, and olive oil (to taste). Mix thoroughly after each addition.

Season with the salt and black pepper.

Sprinkle with the sliced almonds.

Delicious served with Sesame Chicken Balls (see page 39).

carb-loading pasta salad

serves 6–8

1 lb penne pasta—use brown
  pasta for a healthier dish
1½ lb bread-and-butter
  pickles, chopped
14 oz canned tuna

1¼ cups canned corn, drained
⅔ cup low-fat mayonnaise
¼ cup ketchup
salt and black pepper to taste

Cook the pasta according to the package instructions and drain. (Do not overcook it.)

Leave the pasta to cool.

Add the bread-and-butter pickles, tuna, and corn.

Mix the mayonnaise and ketchup together to make a Marie Rose dressing.

Mix into the above ingredients and season to taste.

This recipe is very quick and easy to do. Make sure you always keep these ingredients in your pantry for those surprise lunch guests.

chinese duck salad

serves 6

1 large duck
1 onion, peeled
1 teaspoon garlic purée
¼ lb mixed salad leaves
1 mango, cubed
¼ lb blanched peanuts
¼ lb sugar-snap peas, blanched
¼ lb bean sprouts
ready-made plum sauce
salt and black pepper to taste

for the dressing
1 teaspoon ground ginger
2 tablespoons brown sugar
1 teaspoon dijon mustard
1 tablespoon clear honey
1¼ cups no-pulp orange juice

Preheat the oven to 375°F.

Prick the duck all over with a fork. Put the onion and garlic purée in the duck's cavity, then place the duck on a rack over a roasting pan and cook in the preheated oven for two hours, or until the meat is done, turning the bird over every 30 minutes. Drain off any liquid that collects in the pan. Leave the duck to cool.

Prepare the dressing by mixing all the dressing ingredients together.

Shred the duck meat.

In a serving bowl, place the salad leaves, mango cubes, peanuts, sugar-snap peas, bean sprouts, and duck meat. Pour on the dressing, toss, then season to taste.

Drizzle the plum sauce over the top just before serving.

It is so much easier to buy a cooked duck!

parsley potato salad

serves 6

24 new potatoes
   (allow 4 per person)
1 bunch of flat-leaf parsley
juice of 1 lemon

virgin olive oil
1 cup black pitted olives, sliced
salt and black pepper to taste

Wash the potatoes and place them in a saucepan. Cover with water, bring to a boil, then turn down the temperature and simmer until the potatoes are cooked (not too soft—just so a knife will easily cut through).

Drain the potatoes and allow them to cool.

Add the chopped parsley, the lemon juice, a good drizzle of virgin olive oil, and the olives.

Season to taste.

A lovely way of making a healthier potato salad instead of a cholesterol-loaded killer!

roasted vegetable salad with goat cheese

serves 6–8

8 carrots, peeled and cut
  into thin strips
8 parsnips, peeled and cut
  into thin strips
2 sweet potatoes, peeled and
  cut into thin strips
2 eggplants, peeled and cut
  into thin strips

virgin olive oil
sea salt
1 bunch fresh cilantro, chopped
1 handful of walnuts (optional)
3 oz soft goat cheese

Preheat the oven to 350°F.

Place all the prepared vegetables in a roasting pan.

Drizzle with the olive oil.

Sprinkle with the sea salt.

Roast in the preheated oven for 45 minutes, turning the vegetables halfway through cooking.

Remove from the oven and allow to cool.

Place the vegetables into a large bowl. Add the chopped cilantro and walnuts (if using).

Spoon in small balls of the goat cheese.

Drizzle with more virgin olive oil, if desired.

If you don't like goat cheese, use mozzarella balls instead.

tuscan tomato salad

serves 6

4 beefsteak tomatoes, sliced
about 25 small tomatoes (such as
    santa: sweet grape tomatoes),
    cut in half
6 vine tomatoes, sliced
1 red onion, finely chopped
2 bread rolls or a day-old french
    baguette, cubed

1 handful of fresh basil
    leaves, chopped
4 tablespoons virgin olive oil
4 tablespoons balsamic vinegar
salt and black pepper to taste

Combine the tomatoes, onion, bread, and fresh basil leaves.

Add the virgin olive oil and balsamic vinegar to taste.

Season with the salt and pepper.

Let this marinate for at least one hour in the refrigerator before serving. And do try and visit Tuscany for the real thing!

4

soup

soup: a.k.a. jewish penicillin

In my house, we don't have snack time—we have soup time. When my children get home from school, especially in the winter, some sort of soup is always there, ready to warm and comfort them. My children know that when they open the front door, they can smell home!

Yes, soup is the perfect pep-you-up. Which makes it very sad that so many people today never even bother to make it, thinking that it takes a zillion different ingredients and way too much time and effort. But trust me: would a true Jewish Princess include a chapter on soup in her book if that were the case? With all the fantastic vegetable and chicken bouillon cubes and powders* (including kosher) that are so readily available today, there's no need to spend hours making homemade stock (although you can, if you insist). Instead, you just add boiling water and get going—so perfect for Princesses!

The great thing about soup is its versatility. Whether it's served in a bowl or a mug, good soup truly is a lifesaver. Soup is the Jewish equivalent of the British cup of tea. When you are feeling ill, cold or tired, there is nothing like a good, hot bowl of homemade soup. And it doesn't just taste good—it does you good, too. In fact, chicken soup has been scientifically proven to have medicinal healing powers.

No wonder we've called it "Jewish penicillin" for years!

*We JPs never use bouillon cubes as they don't dissolve easily. However, if this is all you have in your pantry, then one bouillon cube is roughly equal to one tablespoon of powdered bouillon.

bean and barley soup

serves 8

1 fowl (chicken; *see page 194*), skinned, cut into eight pieces
3 tablespoons chicken bouillon powder
1 cup canned lentils, rinsed and drained
1½ cups canned butter beans, rinsed and drained
¾ cup pearl barley, rinsed
1 large onion, peeled

4 large carrots, peeled, topped, and tailed and cut into chunks
1 leek, cut into chunks
1 turnip, peeled and chopped
1 whole beefsteak tomato (skin left on)
1 small celeriac (celery root), cubed
1 tablespoon salt
12 grinds of fresh black pepper
about 10 cups of water

Place the cleaned fowl in a large saucepan and add all of the other ingredients.

Bring to a boil, then turn down the heat and let simmer, covered, for at least three hours, or until the chicken meat is falling away from the bone.

Remove the tomato.

When serving, shred the chicken or remove the carcass completely (optional).

This is a meal in a bowl—and it's also low on the glycemic index.

bloody mary borscht

serves 8

12 medium, raw beets,
  peeled and cubed
1 medium onion
1 medium carrot
5 cups hot water mixed with
  2 tablespoons of vegetable
  bouillon powder

3 tablespoons sugar
black pepper to taste
4⅓ cups tomato juice
worcestershire sauce to taste
splash of vodka

Peel the beets and onion; peel, top, and tail the carrot. Place the vegetables in a large saucepan.

Add the water and bouillon mixture, then the sugar, and season with plenty of black pepper.

Bring to a boil, then turn down the heat and simmer until the vegetables are soft. Remove the carrot and onion.

When cooled, add the tomato juice, blend well, then run the liquid through a strainer.

Add the Worcestershire sauce to taste, then the splash of vodka. Refrigerate until ready to serve.

Serve chilled.

When serving this soup, add a little jug of vodka for people to help themselves. This is a fabulous, fun soup—but watch out if you're wearing white...

broccoli soup

serves 6

3 tablespoons unsalted butter
2 medium onions, diced
1½ lb broccoli, trimmed
  and cut into florets
about ½ cup all-purpose flour

5 cups vegetable stock (make this
  with 2 heaped tablespoons of
  vegetable bouillon powder)
1 pinch of nutmeg
salt and pepper to taste
1¼ cups milk

In a large saucepan over a gentle heat, melt the butter, making sure it doesn't burn.

Sauté the chopped onions until soft. Add the broccoli and cook for five minutes, or until just tender.

Stir in the flour and cook gently for one minute. Remove from the heat and gradually stir in the stock.

Bring to a boil and then reduce the heat. Cover and simmer for 15 to 20 minutes, or until the vegetables are tender.

Add the nutmeg. Season to taste with the salt and black pepper.

Put the soup into a food processor or blender and whizz until smooth.

Reheat gently and slowly stir in the milk.

A delicious and creamy soup full of vitamins—and the children won't even realize it!

A Jewish Princess goes into a restaurant
and sees they have fish soup on the menu.
She calls the waiter over and asks:
"Does the fish soup contain shellfish?"
"Yes," says the waiter.
She calls over another waiter and asks:
"Does the fish soup contain shellfish?"
"Yes," says the waiter.
She calls over a third waiter and asks again:
"Does the fish soup contain shellfish?"
"No," says the waiter.

The Jewish Princess replies: "I'll have it!"

no shellfish fish soup

serves 8

1 onion, chopped
4 carrots, peeled, topped, and tailed, then chopped
3 leeks, chopped
2 potatoes, peeled and cubed
2 vegetable bouillon cubes
1 teaspoon curry powder
1 teaspoon cinnamon
1 pinch of saffron, softened in a little boiling water
half a bottle of dry white wine

2 tablespoons brandy
1 carrot, peeled, topped, tailed, and grated
1 leek, cut into thin strips
½ cup plus 2 tablespoons heavy cream
1¼ lb mixed skinless fish fillets (salmon, cod, and haddock), cut into chunks
salt and black pepper to taste

Place the onion, chopped carrots, chopped leeks, and the cubed potatoes into a large saucepan.

Dissolve the vegetable bouillon cubes in 2½ cups of boiling water and pour over the vegetables. Add more water if the vegetables are not covered.

Add the curry powder, cinnamon, and saffron.

Bring to a boil, then turn down the heat and simmer until the vegetables are soft (approximately 20 minutes).

Process the soup with a hand blender.

In a separate saucepan, pour in the wine and brandy and simmer until the liquid starts to reduce.

Add the grated carrot and the leek strips. Cook gently until the vegetables are soft.

Add this mixture to the main soup.

Stir in the heavy cream and add the fish. Cook on a low heat for a further ten minutes, or until the fish is cooked and flaky.

Season to taste with salt and black pepper.

This is delicious served with French bread that has been sliced and toasted with grated Emmental cheese on top and tomato aioli, which is a garlic mayonnaise with a tomato twist.

To make the aioli, just take 4 tablespoons of mayonnaise, add a half-teaspoon of tomato paste, a half-teaspoon of garlic paste, and a half-teaspoon of Dijon mustard, and voilà: it will take you straight to the South of France.

honey-roasted butternut squash soup

serves 8

4½ lb butternut squash (sometimes called winter squash), cut into 3-inch wedges and deseeded
3 tablespoons olive oil
garlic purée
salt and pepper to taste
4 onions, finely chopped

4 carrots, topped, tailed and finely chopped
2 teaspoons dried parsley
4 tablespoons vegetable bouillon powder dissolved in 10 cups of boiling water
1½ tablespoons clear honey

Preheat the oven to 475°F.

Brush the squash wedges with a little olive oil and place them on a roasting pan. Dot the wedges with garlic purée (about one teaspoon per wedge), then season with salt and pepper and roast for 45 minutes in the oven. Cool, then scoop the flesh off the skin.

Heat the three tablespoons of olive oil in a large saucepan. Add the onions and carrots and cook gently for 10 to 15 minutes, or until the vegetables are soft but not brown. Add the parsley.

Pour the vegetable stock onto the vegetables, bring to a boil, then turn down the heat and simmer for 20 minutes, or until tender.

Add the squash to the stock and vegetables. Simmer for five more minutes.

Blend until smooth, stir in the honey, and gently heat through. Check the seasoning and adjust if necessary.

When you cut the butternut squash, be careful: they're very tough-skinned. You don't want to end up in the E.R.!

jerusalem artichoke soup

serves 8

4 tablespoons olive oil
1¼ lb red onions, chopped
1¼ lb potatoes, peeled
  and chopped
2¼ lb jerusalem artichokes
  (sunchokes), peeled
  and chopped

2 tablespoons vegetable
  bouillon powder
5 cups water
salt and black pepper to taste
1¼ cups soy milk

Heat the olive oil in a large saucepan. Add the red onions and cook, stirring constantly, until soft.

Add the potatoes and Jerusalem artichokes, cover, and sweat for ten minutes (this means the vegetables—not you going out for a jog!).

Add the bouillon powder, water, and seasoning. Simmer on a low heat until the vegetables are soft (approximately 30 minutes).

Puree the soup and stir in the soy milk.

Check the seasoning and adjust if necessary.

Don't be scared of Jerusalem artichokes. Underneath the knobbly skin of these unusual, ugly vegetables lies a true delicacy.

leek and potato soup

serves 8

1½ tablespoons olive oil
2 onions, finely chopped
7 large leeks, washed, peeled
  and finely chopped
4 large potatoes, cut into
  half-inch chunks
2 level tablespoons vegetable
  bouillon powder

10 cups water
sea salt and black pepper
  to taste
1 teaspoon ground nutmeg
1¼ cups heavy cream
2 tablespoons fresh
  chives, chopped

In a large saucepan, heat the olive oil. Add the onions and leeks and gently sauté until soft.

Add the potatoes, the vegetable bouillon powder, water, salt, and pepper. Bring to a boil, turn down the heat and simmer, covered, for 20 to 25 minutes, or until the vegetables are soft.

Stir in the nutmeg.

Remove from the heat and allow to cool.

Puree the soup thoroughly and stir in the cream.

Check the seasoning and adjust if necessary.

To serve, stir in a little swirl of cream in each bowl and garnish with chopped chives.

This can be made the day before to allow the flavors to infuse—and to give Jewish Princesses a little extra shopping time.

mushy pea soup

serves 8

4 lb frozen *petits pois* (tiny peas)
  or other green peas
1 large onion, chopped
3 leeks, sliced
1 tablespoon dried parsley

chicken or vegetable bouillon
  powder—approximately
  3 tablespoons
salt and black pepper to taste
mint leaves, for decoration

Place the *petits pois*, onion, and leeks in a large saucepan.
Add the parsley and bouillon powder, fill the saucepan with
enough water to cover the vegetables, then bring to a boil. Turn
down the heat and let simmer, covered, until the peas are very soft.

Puree the soup. Add the salt and pepper to taste.

When the soup has cooled, push it through a strainer—this is
annoying, but it makes the soup taste incredible! To serve, put
a few mint leaves in each bowl for decoration.

*To make a fun "British" dinner, ask your husband to go get some
fish and chips—so now you have your fish, chips, and peas!*

onion soup

serves 6

5 teaspoons olive oil
4 medium onions, sliced
4 teaspoons sugar
7 cups water

3 tablespoons vegetable
 bouillon powder
2 teaspoons worcestershire sauce
2 tablespoons sherry
salt and black pepper to taste

In a large saucepan, heat the olive oil, then add the onions and sweat them until soft.

Add the rest of the ingredients.

Bring to a boil, then lower the heat and cover. Leave the soup to simmer on a very low heat for about 30 minutes.

Season to taste.

When serving, toast thick slices of French bread and melt grated Cheddar or Emmental cheese on them. Chop them up and place them as croutons in the middle of the soup.

parsnip and apple soup

serves 6

1 onion, diced
1 lb parsnips, washed
   and cubed
7 cups boiled water
3 tablespoons vegetable
   bouillon powder

5 eating apples, peeled
   and sliced
1 cup heavy cream

Put the onions, parsnips, water, and bouillon powder in a large saucepan. Bring to a boil, lower the heat, cover, and simmer for 20 minutes, or until the parsnips are soft.

Meanwhile, put the peeled apples in a separate microwavable bowl, cover with two tablespoons of water and cook on high for two minutes. When you take the apples out of the microwave, check that they are soft.

Add the apples to the vegetables.

Liquidize the soup and stir in the cream to serve.

This one will keep your dinner guests guessing, trying to work out all the ingredients.

tomato soup with basil-infused croutons

serves 6

2 tablespoons olive oil
4 shallots, peeled and chopped
3 celery sticks, washed
  and chopped
2 carrots, peeled, topped,
  tailed, and chopped
1 large handful of torn
  basil leaves
1 large bunch of sage leaves
2 bay leaves
42 oz canned chopped
  tomatoes in their juice

5 cups water mixed with
  2 tablespoons of vegetable
  bouillon powder
3½ tablespoons sugar
salt and black pepper to taste
splash of olive oil

for the croutons
day-old french bread
1 garlic clove
6 tablespoons olive oil
1 handful of torn basil leaves

First, make the croutons.

Preheat the oven to 275°F.

Slice the French bread into thin slices. Rub both sides with garlic.

Using a hand blender, blend together the olive oil and basil in
a bowl.

Brush the mixture onto one side of the bread slices.

Place in the preheated oven for 20 minutes, turning halfway
through, until the bread has dried out.

Place in an airtight container.

To make the soup, heat the olive oil in a large saucepan. Add the shallots and sauté.

As they become translucent, add the celery, carrots, basil, sage, and bay leaves.

When the vegetables are soft, add all the other ingredients.

Reduce the heat, cover, and simmer on a low heat for a good hour or so.

Puree the soup.

To make it extra-special, pour it through a strainer before serving.

Serve with the basil-infused croutons.

Tomato soup is hard to get right, but this is JP perfect! Serve with croutons and a basil leaf to decorate.

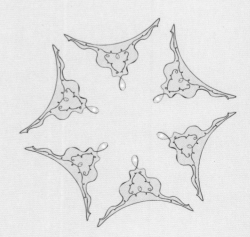

diaspora dishes:
london to new york

And now, an aside. While you recover from all those luscious soups, salads, and appetizers, it's time for a little break before diving into the main courses. So put your feet up for a minute and relax while reading the following. It's educational (well, a *bissel*...).

Maybe it's because of the Jewish people's history of dispersal, traditionally known as the Diaspora, but whatever the reason, the modern Jewish Princess still loves to roam—or should I say Rome, Paris, Milan, London, and New York? Cities like these, after all, are centers of cultural importance, home to resplendent art galleries, shops, magnificent museums, shops, incredible restaurants—and did I mention the most amazing shops?

To a JP, this intoxicating combination is always a recipe for success. Whenever I return from any vacation, I'm always motivated to try out in my own kitchen all the foods I've eaten and loved abroad. Almost as soon as the tires hit the runway, I find myself running to my nearest supermarket to stock up on new foods I have experienced (OK, so I'm in the shops again), simply to bring back the flavor of wherever it is I've just been.

Throughout history, Jewish Princesses have loved to travel, and our food contains tastes and flavors that come from all over the world. This makes Jewish cooking terrifically exciting, as this melting pot of global flavors produces the most extraordinary dishes. From Spain to South Africa, London to Lithuania, Ashkenazi and Sephardi Jews (*see* Yiddish/English Glossary, page 210) have concocted a unique style of cooking that takes a little of this and a little of that to create food which family and friends adore.

So next time you come home from vacation, if you can't fit the sun into your luggage due to the other purchases you made, just remember all those flavors you tasted and savored. With a bit of culinary creativity, you can be transported back to that special place again and again.

5

meat

meat: not always a "rare" kosher treat

No matter how far she may wander or roam, ultimately a Jewish Princess will have to make some key decisions.

The first is: "Do I keep a kosher home?"
The second: "Do I keep kosher when I go out to eat?"
The third: "Do I eat only in kosher restaurants, or eat only certain fish or vegetarian dishes and go to non-kosher restaurants?"

Everyone finds her own level. Often it relates to how you were brought up or how guilty (ever heard of Jewish guilt?) you might feel if your fork touched a forbidden food. For a Jewish Princess, it is up to her to find which foods may turn her into a frog.

I made my decision and decided to keep a kosher home. Therefore the relationship I have with my butcher is of paramount importance. Not, obviously, as important as the relationship I have with my hairdresser, but close.

I have spent many years searching for an excellent butcher. This search was a bit like my dating years. I have "courted" a few butchers in my time, but I had to dump them for various reasons: sending me a hairy chicken; not saving me eggs for the chicken soup (a great kosher delicacy—these golden eggs are in short supply and I am not prepared to do my butcher any favors to get them). A tough piece of beef was definitely a dumping offence, but the worst crime of all was when a butcher completely ripped me off for a crown roast of lamb by charging me an exorbitant price.

I'm afraid there was A Scene.

Finally, however, after much cruising and schmoozing, I found the perfect butcher. Of course, we are on first-name terms; I know all about his family, (well, most of them work in the shop). My chickens are hairless, my beef is always tender and delicious, and he always saves me the precious golden eggs for my chicken soup—*without* any favors!

Why am I telling you all this? Simple: my friends and family are Carnivores, with a capital "C." We just *love* meat.

Also, many of my friends have made the decision to keep kosher when eating out, and they will eat only fish and vegetarian dishes in non-kosher restaurants. They spend their evenings eyeing up pieces of beef and chicken that come flying out of the kitchen and past them, carried by deaf waiters. (Don't you find that this is a common affliction affecting most waiters? It seems to be a requirement for the job...) So when my kosher-keeping friends come to my home for dinner, it is a really special treat to indulge in meat—and there is nothing more satisfying than to take a juicy roast out of the oven and know that my guests will truly appreciate it.

Now I realize that, like fine wine, there is a certain amount of snobbery regarding the cooking of meat, but I have to say, give the people what they want. If they don't like it rare now, they never will. And if they love it well-done, then you should serve it that way.

It is the *enjoyment* of the meat that is everything.

So when I have guests, there are no deaf waiters (I do occasionally have a waitress, but that's only for very large gatherings), the meat is always cooked to my friends' requirements, and when I see an empty plate I know that I, for one, will get a big "well done."

A Jewish Princess went on a
walking tour. She power-walked
from Egypt to Israel.

It took her forty years, but boy,
did she have great legs by the end!

chicken curry in a hurry

serves 2

3 tablespoons olive oil
2 onions, diced
2 boneless chicken breasts, diced
6 oz canned tomatoes
   in tomato juice
3 teaspoons medium
   curry powder

2 oz or a generous ⅓ cup
   sultanas (golden or white raisins)
1 banana, sliced
¾ cup canned coconut cream
1 teaspoon sugar
salt and pepper to taste
mango chutney to serve

Heat a wok or a large, heavy frying pan.

Add the olive oil.

Add the chopped onions and sauté until brown, then add the diced chicken and stir until cooked.

Add the tomatoes and curry powder to taste, then stir in the sultanas and the sliced banana and cook for approximately three minutes.

Add the coconut cream and the sugar and continue cooking until the liquid has reduced and a creamy sauce is left (approximately ten minutes).

Season to taste with salt and pepper.

Serve with cooked rice and mango chutney on the side for a hot, romantic dinner for two.

chicken schnitzel in wine and spritely lemonade

serves 10

10 boneless chicken breasts
3 large eggs, beaten
breadcrumbs or matzo meal
olive oil, for frying

for the marinade
¾ cup white wine
½ cup sprite
4 garlic cloves, crushed
2 tablespoons lemon juice
4–5 tablespoons chopped
    fresh chives

Mix all the marinade ingredients together and pour over the chicken breasts. Leave to marinate for a couple of hours—or even better, overnight.

Dip the chicken breasts into the beaten egg, then into the bread crumbs or matzo meal.

Fry in the olive oil until golden brown and serve.

This unusual concoction always goes down well, even with picky eaters. Try it and see!

gedempte chicken

serves 6

3 tablespoons corn oil
1 red onion, diced
1 white onion, diced
1 chicken, cut into 8 pieces
enough all-purpose flour
  to coat the chicken
2¼ cups water
16 oz passata (smooth, thick,

sieved tomatoes; if unavailable,
  use tomato puree)
2 garlic cloves, pressed
2 bouquets garni
salt and black pepper to taste
6 large potatoes, cut into quarters
  and parboiled

Heat the oil and fry the onions in a large wok or frying pan until they are as dark as possible without burning them.

Dip the chicken pieces in the flour and fry them with the onions until the chicken is slightly brown.

Transfer the chicken and onions into a deep saucepan and add the water, passata (or puree), garlic, the bouquets garni, salt and pepper.

Bring to the boil, then turn down the heat, cover, and let it simmer very gently until the chicken is soft and dark brown in color. This will take at least one and a half hours.

Halfway through the cooking, add the partly boiled potatoes, which will continue to cook in the meat juices and will turn a dark brown.

Whenever I make this, I feel like my grandmother-over-shalom is with us at the table, enjoying the fact that all the family are together.

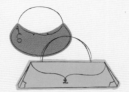

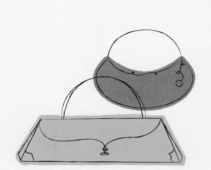

A Jewish Princess goes into
the butcher shop to pick up
her chickens.

"Are they in yet?" she inquires.

"No," says the butcher. "They'll
be back from the dry cleaners in
two minutes!"

moroccan chicken

serves 6

vegetable oil, enough to fry
   (approximately 4 tablespoons)
1 tablespoon tomato purée
2 teaspoons garlic purée
2 teaspoons cumin
1 teaspoon cinnamon
1 chicken, cut into 8 pieces

4 medium onions, peeled and
   sliced (use frozen if you like)
18 dried apricots
1¼ cups water
1 tablespoon chicken bouillon
   powder (or 1 bouillon cube)
salt and black pepper to taste

Preheat the oven to 350°F.

Heat the vegetable oil, then add the tomato purée, garlic purée, cumin, and cinnamon.

Quickly fry each piece of chicken.

Place the chicken pieces in a roasting pan.

Fry the onions in the remaining oil until they are soft. Do not burn!

Pour the onions over the chicken.

Add the dried apricots and water mixed with the chicken bouillon powder (or cube) to the bottom of the roasting pan. Season with the salt and pepper.

Roast in the preheated oven for at least one hour, or until the juices run clear.

Delicious served with couscous. Just don't do those belly-dancing exercises straight afterwards…

poussin with apple and sage

serves 6

3 poussin (if unavailable, use
   small cornish hens); allow at
   least half a poussin per person
3 gala (or similar) apples, halved
6 fresh sage leaves per poussin
shallots, peeled
carrots, topped, tailed, peeled,
   and cut into chunks

chicken bouillon, approximately
   2¼ cups
salt and black pepper to taste
honey
olive oil
fresh oregano leaves

Preheat the oven to 350°F.

Clean each poussin.

Stuff each one with two apple halves and six sage leaves.

In the bottom of a roasting pan, place the peeled whole shallots
and peeled chunks of carrots (as many as you want).

Place the poussin in the roasting dish and pour in enough chicken
bouillon so that the dish is at least half full.

Season the poussin with salt and black pepper. Rub a little honey
and olive oil into the skin of each poussin.

Sprinkle fresh oregano leaves over the top.

Roast in the preheated oven for 45 to 60 minutes, or until the skin
is golden.

*This is easy to make and serve, and the result looks like a
professional chef has invaded your kitchen.*

cumberland cutlets

serves 4–6 *(depending on how many men you're serving!)*

8 lamb cutlets
salt and pepper to season
2 medium eggs, beaten
fine matzo meal or
   fine breadcrumbs

for the sauce
2 cups chicken bouillon
9 rounded tablespoons red currant
   (or cranberry) jelly
juice of 4 oranges
1 orange, sliced, for garnish
5 teaspoons lemon juice

Preheat the oven to 400°F.

Trim off most of the fat from the lamb cutlets, then sprinkle with salt and pepper.

Dip the cutlets into the beaten egg, then into the breadcrumbs or matzo meal. Put in a baking dish or roasting pan side by side.

To make the sauce, heat all the ingredients together until smooth and pour half over the cutlets. Cover with foil.

Cook in the preheated oven for one hour, then add the remaining sauce. Turn the oven down to 350°F and cook for an additional 20 minutes.

Garnish with the orange segments.

Not, sadly, named after the Cumberland Hotel in Bournemouth, England: a kosher hotel that existed in the 1970s and one that was renowned for its copious amounts of food.

sticky lamb chops

serves 6

⅓ cup clear honey
⅓ cup ketchup
⅓ cup dark soy sauce

⅓ cup water
12 medium lamb chops

Combine the honey, ketchup, soy sauce, and water in a bowl.

Arrange the lamb chops side by side in an ovenproof dish.

Pour the sauce over the meat and place in the fridge to marinate for half an hour (or longer if desired).

When ready to cook, bake uncovered in an oven preheated to 325°F for at least an hour.

Check that the chops are not drying out, and turn throughout cooking, basting with the marinade.

A favorite with Junior JPs.

shepherd's pie

serves 6

1 onion, diced
1½ teaspoons non-dairy margarine
½ lb mushrooms,
   peeled and sliced
1 lb ground lamb
14.5 oz can of chopped tomatoes
6 bay leaves
salt and black pepper to taste

for the topping
2¼ lb sweet potatoes,
   peeled and diced
2 tablespoons non-dairy margarine
1 tablespoon tomato purée
½ teaspoon cumin
½ teaspoon nutmeg
salt and black pepper to taste

Fry the onion in the margarine until slightly brown.

Add the mushrooms and continue to fry until soft.

Add the meat, the canned tomatoes, and the bay leaves and simmer on a low heat for one hour. Don't forget to season with salt and black pepper at this point!

Transfer the lamb to an ovenproof dish.

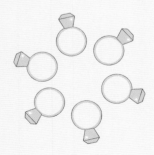

Next, make the topping. Put the sweet potatoes in a saucepan with just enough water to cover, then boil them until soft.

Drain off the water and leave the potatoes to cool.

Preheat the oven to 375°F.

Add the rest of the topping ingredients to the potatoes and mash thoroughly. Spread the topping over the cooked lamb.

Bake the lamb in the preheated oven for approximately 25 minutes, or until the topping has become crispy.

When you make this dish you won't need a shepherd to get everyone to the table!

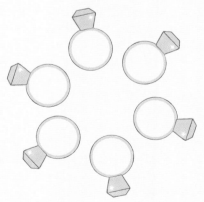

brisket with prunes

serves 6

3¼ lb brisket (unpickled)
2 parsnips
6 carrots
2 onions

black pepper to taste
1 bay leaf
12 dried pitted prunes
2 oz onion soup mix

Preheat the oven to 300°F.

Wash the brisket and place the meat in a roasting pan filled halfway with water.

Peel all the vegetables and leave them whole. Season well with black pepper and add them to the roasting pan.

Add the rest of the ingredients.

Cover with foil and cook in the preheated oven for three hours, turning the brisket every hour, until the meat is soft.

A great dish for impressing your guests, especially when served with couscous. As a bonus, you can leave it in the oven and have a little "me time" (three hours' worth!) before they arrive.

you say corned beef, i say salt beef

serves 8

4½ lb center pickled brisket
1 onion, washed but not peeled
6 peppercorns

1 bay leaf, split either end
  to infuse
1 teaspoon sugar

Place the washed brisket in a large saucepan and cover with water. Cover with the pan lid and bring to a boil.

When scum appears, throw away the first water and refill with fresh, clean, cold water—enough to cover the beef.

Add the onion, peppercorns, bay leaf, and sugar and bring to a boil.

When scum reappears, skim this away with a large spoon. Place the lid half on the saucepan and continue to simmer for approximately two and a half hours, or until the beef is tender.

Add boiling water to the saucepan if the liquid falls below the line of the beef.

To see if the beef has cooked, test it by piercing with a fork. If it comes out easily, it's ready.

Either serve immediately or allow the beef to get cold.

When cold, slice thinly and reheat in the microwave with a little of the juices on top.

For a great sandwich, deli-style, serve salt beef on rye bread with English mustard and pickles. Salt beef and latkes (see page 41) are the Jewish "eggs and bacon."

cholent
(meat stew with legumes and potatoes)

serves 8

4½ lb stewing beef
6 onions, sliced
1 scant cup pearl barley
6 large potatoes, cut into quarters
2 bay leaves
¾ cup (drained) canned
  cannellini beans
¾ cup (drained) canned
  butter beans
¾ cup (drained) canned
  borlotti (cranberry) beans (use
  pinto beans if unavailable)

12 oz passata (smooth, thick,
  sieved tomatoes; if unavailable,
  use tomato puree)
plenty of black pepper
2 teaspoons salt
2 teaspoons dark brown sugar
3 carrots, peeled, topped,
  and tailed
2 tablespoons beef bouillon
  powder (or 2 cubes)

Preheat the oven to 400°F.

Place all the ingredients in a large, heavy, ovenproof pot or dish (I use a large saucepan), with the beef in the center and the potatoes around the beef.

Pour in enough water to cover all the ingredients, then cover and cook in the preheated oven for one hour.

Turn the heat down to 300°F and leave in the oven for the next seven hours.

If you're going to leave the dish to cook longer, just turn the heat down even more.

I know this breaks the ten-ingredient rule, but it's allowed due to the fact that it is simply a matter of opening cans (just watch your fingernails, of course!).

This wonderful stew is traditionally made on Friday before the Sabbath, and left in the oven overnight, ready for lunch the next day. Absolutely delicious.

tzimmes
(braised beef and carrots)

serves *as many as you like!*

2¼ lb carrots, peeled
    and cubed (or buy prepared)
3 tablespoons light brown sugar
beef brisket or rolled rib (any size,
    depending on how many you
    want to feed)
salt and pepper to taste
olive oil, for searing

4 tablespoons cornstarch
2¼ lb potatoes, peeled and
    sliced thickly
1⅓ cups golden syrup
    (if unavailable, use ⅔ cup each
    of honey and light corn syrup,
    although the taste will be
    slightly different)

Preheat the oven to 275°F.

Boil the carrots until *al dente* in water to which one tablespoon
of brown sugar has been added.

Season the meat with salt and pepper.

Coat a large frying pan with a little oil, heat it, and sear
the meat.

In a bowl, put two tablespoons of brown sugar and two
tablespoons of cornstarch. Stir them together.

Drain the carrots, reserving the liquid.

Line a large, deep, heatproof casserole with a layer of carrots.
Sprinkle them with the sugar and cornstarch mixture.

Place the seared meat on top of the carrots in the middle of
the casserole.

Sprinkle two tablespoons of cornstarch over the meat.

Continue layering with carrots and potatoes, seasoning each layer as you go.

Pour the reserved carrot liquid into the casserole, making sure the meat is covered. Add water if needed.

Pour in the golden syrup, then cover the dish tightly with aluminum foil to keep it from drying out.

Cook in the preheated oven for at least eight hours. Keep checking to see if it needs some more water.

This dish is best made the day before so that you can leave it to cook overnight on a low heat. It's great to serve in front of the fire on a cold, dark evening with a big glass of red wine.

ye olde steak pie

serves 6

2¼ lb diced steak
½ lb button mushrooms
1 oz onion soup mix
½ cup plus 2 tablespoons kiddush
  wine (or you can use
  your favorite cooking red)
½ cup plus 2 tablespoons water
1 garlic clove
6 shallots, peeled
  and left whole

4 small (or 2 large) carrots,
  topped, tailed, and chopped
14.5 oz canned chopped
  tomatoes
1 teaspoon sugar
black pepper to taste

for the pastry
1 lb puff pastry
1 medium egg, lightly whisked

Preheat the oven to 250°F.

Place all the casserole ingredients in a round casserole dish.

Cover with a lid or foil, and cook slowly in the oven for at least three hours, or until the meat is soft.

Leave to cool. Check the seasoning and adjust if necessary.

Roll out the pastry (unless you buy pastry already rolled—great move, I say!).

Paint beaten egg around the rim of the casserole. Add the pastry and press down the sides to seal.

Brush beaten egg over the top and make a cross in the center with your knife (this stops the pastry from going soggy).

Preheat the oven to 425°F and bake for five minutes, then reduce the heat to 375°F and bake for a further 30 minutes, until the gravy is bubbling up.

If you're concerned about the pastry (especially if you're watching your carbs), just make the casserole by itself.

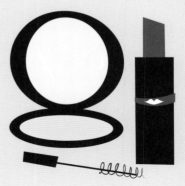

6

fish

f.i.s.h. = finally i saved him

After Hubby and I had been going out for a few weeks, I was sure he would be ready to propose once he had been to our house for a Friday night dinner.

This, of course, led to the inevitable problem of having to consider that maybe it wasn't *me* he fell in love with, but the meal my mother served him...

But anyway.

The reason I felt I was on to a sure thing was simple. Because his mother, for some very bizarre reason, served fish on Friday nights (maybe she thought they were Catholic?), Hubby had been deprived of the joys of chicken soup, chopped liver, and roast chicken all his life (*see* "The Ultimate Friday Night Dinner," page 187). So when he arrived at my house and saw the table, when he was served piping-hot chicken soup and all the rest, he saw in my mother the promise of the woman I would become.

That night, instead of eating it, Hubby-To-Be *turned into* fish. He had been well and truly caught!

Due to the fish that was forced upon him, my lovely husband suffered for many years with a fish phobia. After all, if *you* had been given fish that looked like it had just escaped from a hospital ward (his mother wasn't the most imaginative cook), you, too, would find yourself fearing fish.

So Hubby hated fish with a passion, and whenever he had to eat at his mother's after we were married, she just served him a hard-boiled egg, since, by this time, she had finally given up. (Being a true Jewish Princess, I always politely ate my hospital fare.)

Because of his fish fear, I decided that fish should not be forced back into my husband's life. However, I didn't want to deprive myself or my children of that excellent brain food. After all, they would have school exams to take, so they would need every little bit of help they could get (including the odd hour or two of private tutoring—competition is very high).

So with a few clever recipes, I was sure that my beloved could grow to have a fondness for fish. Slowly, over the years, and with the aim of preserving my husband's heart muscle, I have managed—with patience, coaxing, and little phrases such as, "Come on: just one tiny little bite" (well, you know all men are little boys at heart)—to persuade him to eat fish.

And yes, you better believe it: now he actually *likes* it!

It really took some Princess perseverance, but after all, he *was* my soul mate. I knew that, with the right treatment, he could find a plaice—sorry, make that *place*—in his heart for fish.

So if you have a member of your family who says, "I hate x,y, and z," don't give up. After all, at first sight sushi takes some getting used to; now people are in love with it the world over.

I mean, whoever thought *my* Prince would actually *challish* for a piece of raw salmon?

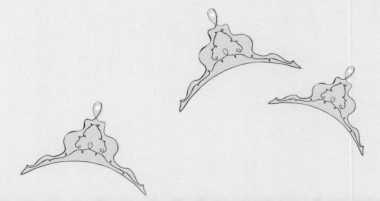

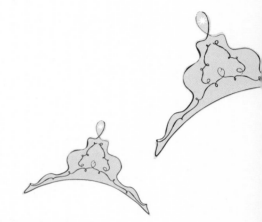

What's a Jewish Princess's
favorite wine?

I want to go to Miami!

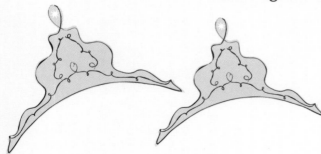

fish tempura

serves 4

1 skinless salmon fillet
(approximately 10–11 oz)
1 skinless cod fillet (approximately
10–11 oz)
salt and black pepper to taste
1¼ cups tempura batter mix
(this can be purchased at
most large supermarkets or
a japanese food store)

vegetable oil
16 baby corn pieces or
baby carrots
soy sauce

Cut each piece of salmon and cod into eight strips.

Season the fish with salt and black pepper.

Mix up the tempura batter.

Coat the fish with tempura batter and fry (making sure there is enough oil to cover the fish) until golden brown.

Coat the vegetables in the batter and fry until golden brown.

Place all the fish and vegetables on paper towels to soak up any excess oil.

Serve with soy sauce on the side to dip.

If you have chopsticks in the house, use these instead of knives and forks—it's much more fun!

haddock kedgeree

serves 4

1 skinless natural smoked haddock
  fillet (approximately 10–11 oz)
1 tablespoon vegetable
  bouillon powder
1¾ cups rice
½ cup unsalted butter

1 teaspoon curry powder
1 handful of chopped parsley
3 medium hard-boiled
  eggs, chopped
2 cups heavy cream
salt and black pepper to taste

Halve the haddock, place in a large saucepan, and cover with water.

Add the vegetable bouillon powder, and cook over a low heat until the haddock is poached.

Remove the fish and leave to cool. Retain the fish stock, but set aside one ladle of it for later.

Add the rice to the fish stock and cook, adding more water if necessary. Set aside when cooked.

Over medium heat, melt ¼ cup of butter in another saucepan. Add the curry powder, chunked haddock, and parsley and sauté gently, stirring constantly.

Add half the cooked rice and keep stirring. Add the remainder of the rice and the rest of the butter. Keep stirring.

Add the chopped egg, the ladle of fish stock, and the cream.

Season to taste with salt and black pepper and serve immediately.

Haddock kedgeree is a bit like garlic—you love it or you hate it. So be careful who you serve it to!

hot and spicy fish

serves 6

for the fish balls
2 large eggs
1 large potato (approximately
   ½ lb), peeled and boiled
   until soft
1 tablespoon dried parsley
1 teaspoon paprika
1 teaspoon ground nutmeg
1 red onion, diced
1 teaspoon garlic purée
1 lb white fish,
   very finely chopped
salt and pepper to taste

for the sauce
28 oz canned chopped tomatoes
about 1⅓ cups chopped
   fresh basil
1 tablespoon tomato purée
2 teaspoons curry powder
2 teaspoons sugar
salt and pepper to taste
3 tablespoons light cream

corn oil, for frying

Place all the fish-ball ingredients in a food processor and process until everything is well-mixed.

Let the mixture rest for 15 minutes.

To make the fish balls, wet your hands with water, then take a heaped teaspoon of the mixture and shape it into an oval.

In a frying pan, fry the fish balls in just enough corn oil to cover until they are a golden color.

Drain on paper towels to absorb any excess oil, then place in an ovenproof dish.

To make the sauce, put all the sauce ingredients into a food processor and mix thoroughly.

Preheat the oven to 350°F.

Pour the sauce over the fish balls and bake in the preheated oven for 40 minutes.

These are great without the sauce to serve with drinks. Or instead of serving them as a main course, serve a smaller amount as a forspeise (see Yiddish/English Glossary, page 210).

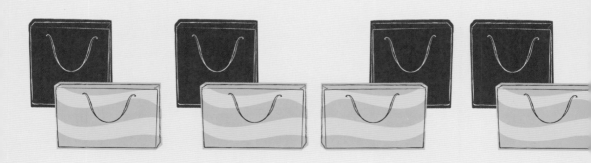

individual salmon en croûte

serves 4

¾ cup heavy cream
9 oz canned asparagus
1 bunch watercress, chopped
1 bunch of dill, chopped
1 pinch of nutmeg
salt and black pepper to taste

1 lb ready-made puff pastry
2 skinless salmon fillets
    (approximately 10 oz each),
    cut in half
1 medium egg, beaten

Preheat the oven to 425°F.

In a large bowl, add the cream, asparagus, chopped watercress, chopped dill, nutmeg, salt, and pepper (season well). Mix with a hand blender.

Roll out the pastry to about a ¼-inch thickness.

Season the salmon with a little salt, then place it on the pastry. Cut a square large enough to cover the salmon and make a parcel.

Spoon the asparagus mixture on top of the salmon and close the pastry to make the parcel. Press down the edges.

Brush on the beaten egg and score the top of the pastry.

Place on waxed paper.

Bake in the preheated oven for 10 to 15 minutes.

If you do not wish to use individual fillets, just use a larger piece of salmon, or make smaller ones to serve as canapés. Once the salmon en croûte is cooked, slice it into pieces to serve.

lemon fish cakes

serves 6

2 medium eggs
4 slices of white bread,
   without crusts
1 tablespoon dried parsley
1 teaspoon hot paprika
1 teaspoon ground nutmeg
1 garlic clove, chopped

1 tablespoon whole-grain mustard
1 tablespoon lemon juice
1 lb white fish, finely chopped
salt and black pepper

corn oil, for frying
mango chutney, for serving

Put all the ingredients, except the oil and chutney, into a food processor and process until they are all well-mixed.

Let the mixture rest for 15 minutes.

Using a heaped teaspoon, drop a spoonful of the mixture at a time into enough oil to cover the cakes and fry until they are golden in color.

Serve on a bed of basmati rice with mango chutney.

paella miami

serves 6

2 tablespoons vegetable oil,
  for frying
1 green chili, deseeded
  and diced
1 medium red pepper, deseeded
  and chopped
2 teaspoons garlic purée
2 large beef tomatoes, sliced
  and cubed
5¼ cups vegetable or fish stock
2 generous pinches of saffron
1 fresh salmon fillet
  (approximately 7–8 oz)

1 fresh cod fillet
  (approximately 10 oz)
1¾ cups rice
1 fresh tuna fillet
  (approximately 6 oz)
4 oz black olives, pitted
  and drained
salt and black pepper to taste
½ lb frozen peas
1 red onion, peeled and sliced
  into rings

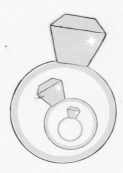

Coat a large, deep frying pan with the vegetable oil (I usually use a wok), then add the chili, pepper, and garlic and cook for five minutes over moderate heat, stirring the ingredients continuously.

Next, add the tomatoes and continue stirring for another five minutes.

Pour in the stock along with the saffron and simmer for ten minutes, keeping an eye on the mixture by stirring occasionally.

Add all the fish except the tuna and simmer for another ten minutes.

Add the rice to the pan, mix it in with the contents, and simmer for another ten minutes.

Add the tuna, salt, and pepper, and olives and cook for a further five minutes.

Add the peas and cook for a further five minutes.

In a separate frying pan, sauté the onion rings in a little olive oil and add on top of the paella to garnish.

So I know this recipe breaks the ten-ingredient rule, but even JPs know that rules are meant to be broken. This dish is so easy to make and looks FABULOUS! Mucho delicious!

sole colbert

serves 2

4 lemon sole (or other
   flounder) fillets (approximately
   1/4 lb each)
salt and black pepper
flour, for dusting

2 bananas, sliced horizontally
1/2 cup unsalted butter
1 tablespoon vegetable oil
mango chutney, to serve

Wash and dry the sole fillets.

Season with salt and black pepper.

Put the flour on a plate and lightly dip the sole fillets into it, then pat off any surplus.

Dip the bananas in the flour, also patting off any surplus.

Heat a frying pan and melt the butter with the oil.

Fry the sole fillets gently, making sure that both sides are brown.

Do the same with the bananas.

Arrange on a plate, with the mango chutney on the side.

Husbands, boyfriends, and lovers will adore this dish. Just don't invite them all over at the same time...

A Jewish Princess
went fishing.

She came home with
a new place!

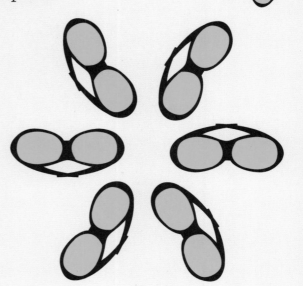

sophisticated fish pie

serves 8

2 onions, diced
2–3 tablespoons vegetable oil
2 eggplants, cubed
4 carrots, topped, tailed,
  and cubed
half a cauliflower, cut into florets
28 oz canned chopped tomatoes
1 cup heavy cream
3 teaspoons curry powder
1 teaspoon ground ginger
2 tablespoons sugar
salt and black pepper
1 smoked skinless haddock fillet,
  (approximately 10 oz), cubed

1 skinless haddock fillet
  (approximately 10 oz), cubed
1 skinless salmon fillet
  (approximately 1 lb), cubed

for the topping
5 medium potatoes, peeled
  and cubed
4 sweet potatoes, peeled
  and cubed
½ cup heavy cream
½ cup unsalted butter
1 teaspoon table salt

Sauté the onions in the vegetable oil in a large saucepan. When they begin to brown, add the eggplant and carrots, and a few minutes later add the cauliflower florets.

When the vegetables have softened, add the canned tomatoes, heavy cream, spices, sugar, salt, and pepper. Simmer for five minutes.

Add the fish and cook for ten minutes.

Next, make the topping. In a separate saucepan, cover the potatoes and sweet potatoes with water, bring to a boil, then reduce the heat and simmer until the vegetables are very soft.

Remove from the heat and drain.

Preheat the oven to 325°F.

Add the cream, butter, and salt, then mash well.

Place the fish mixture in an ovenproof dish (I use a casserole saucepan, which I can just transfer from stove-top to oven).

Add the topping and cook in the preheated oven for 15 to 20 minutes, until bubbling.

A Jewish Princess alternative to oysters and Champagne.

sweet-and-sour halibut

serves 4

4 halibut fillets (approximately
   6–8 oz each)
1 onion
3 bay leaves
salt and pepper

4 medium eggs
2 lemons, juiced
3½ tablespoons sugar
cucumber, for decoration

Place the fish in a saucepan along with the onion, bay leaves, salt, and pepper. Cover with water and bring to a boil.

Simmer for 15 minutes.

When the fish is flaky, take 1 cup of the stock out and strain into a bowl. Allow to cool.

Carefully take out the fish, carefully remove any skin, and place the fish in a deep, heatproof glass dish.

Beat the eggs and add lemon juice to the egg mixture.

Put this on a low heat, and slowly add the fish stock and sugar to taste. Keep stirring for at least 10 to 15 minutes.

When the mixture has thickened, pour it over the cooled fish.

Slice a cucumber thinly and use to decorate the dish.

This vintage recipe is like a good Gucci bag—it will never go out of date.

thai tuna

serves 4

2 large, fresh tuna steaks
   (approximately 8–10 oz
   each), halved
juice of 2 limes
1 bunch of cilantro,
   finely chopped
1 bunch of flat-leaf parsley,
   finely chopped
1 teaspoon lemongrass paste
   (available in most
   good supermarkets)

½ teaspoon garlic purée
half a green chili, chopped
   (if you like it hot, just use
   a whole chili)
half a red pepper, finely chopped
6 cherry tomatoes, quartered
rock salt and black pepper
   to season
olive oil

Place the tuna in a large bowl.

Squeeze on the lime juice, then add the rest of the ingredients
(except the olive oil) and season to taste with salt and black
pepper.

Leave to marinate for one hour.

Coat a griddle or frying pan with olive oil, heat, then add the
tuna and sear each side.

*Great for lunch with the girls—especially if your friends are doing
no carbs!*

weights and measures

A Jewish Princess loves looking good. When you are thin, slim—whatever you want to call it—you're able to choose any jeans you want. If you're not lucky enough to be born with the skinny gene, then as every Princess knows, you've just got to work at it.

You can always try a tapeworm (I've heard of a supplier), or knock back a concoction of dubious herbal pills, hard-core drugs, colonic irrigation, and, as a last resort, liposuction. I've even heard of people trying to *think* themselves thin, but whenever I think of that four-letter word "diet," I just think "food."

However, just like when choosing a handbag, when it comes to eating, I am *selective*. In restaurants I have been known to throw my fork down in disgust at some overly sweet or gelatinous dessert, but for fabulous food I am prepared to throw calorie caution to the wind.

Some Princesses may be in denial, but we all know that the only way to fit into those designer dresses is EXERCISE. Whether running around the shops, hitting the gym, or trying to swim with your head two feet above water (to protect your hair, of course), MOVING (yourself, that is, not changing your address) is the key to keeping your body from going south.

However, I love my food, and I am prepared to exercise my body so that I can exercise my mouth. From the number of other JPs I bump into at the gym, they've discovered this secret, too. Truth be known, I actually *love* exercise; from spinning to stepping, dancing to Pilates, you will find me doing my thaang! I find that all forms of exercise—and I mean *all* forms (except housework)—provide wonderful therapy. Exercise clears the mind, clears the cellulite, and clears away the guilt that rears its ugly head whenever my fork finds that cheesecake.

All this talk of exercise has made me build up quite an appetite, so what better subject to talk about now than delicious desserts? Before we start, though, I think we should finish with one last exercise: flex your fingers and turn the page...

7

desserts

desserts to die-t for!

I think everyone has a dessert they adore, a dessert they cannot turn down. If my son, for example, just so much as sniffs my Choca-challah Pudding (*see* page 134) baking in the oven, I'll find him prowling around the kitchen, waiting. *Challah* is delicious doughy bread made from eggs and is traditionally eaten on a Friday night. However, if there's any left over, my son gives me that puppy-dog look and I know that I will once again be whisking up eggs, chocolate, and cream to make his favorite.

My own weakness is for ice cream. I just love it! I even get pleasure merely from *thinking* about it, and I get quite excited about a new, special flavor. Ice cream has this unique smooth, cold, soft, melting texture that is amazing—and because it is so naughty, it is *soooooo* nice.

My relationship with ice cream once landed me in a spot of trouble.

I was entertaining some rather important clients and, due to nerves, had polished off a little too much of the pink stuff. When it came to dessert, I tottered in (high, high stilettos, naturally) with my magnificent tower of different-flavored ice cream served in a giant brandy basket. One new, exciting flavor I had conjured up was Honey Halva Ice Cream (*see* page 138). *Halva* is a Middle Eastern delicacy made from sesame seeds which has a wonderful ability to stick to the roof of your mouth. Its unusual flavor combined with honey and made into ice cream is a winner. So it's no wonder that, in my eagerness to dive into my own dessert, I didn't wait a second before trying to serve it—and consequently could not prise the balls apart. Up shot a golden ball into the air and landed in the client's lap. I rushed over to help and found myself fumbling in said client's crotch. Scooping up the ball, I held it aloft like a triumphant baseball player and served it to his wife, who ate it. Oh, dear!

Life is short. If you eat too much ice cream, life will be shorter. However, if you strike the right balance of "moderation in everything," as my grandpa used to say, then indulging in your dessert fantasies should be encouraged, especially if it's a dessert to DIE-T for!

baked alaska

serves 6

1 box lady fingers or
    sponge-cake fingers
    (approximately 22)
marsala wine or brandy

the whites of 4 large eggs
1 1/2 cups sugar
2–2 1/4 cups vanilla ice cream
1 oz sliced almonds (optional)

Preheat the oven to 400°F.

Place the lady fingers or sponge-cake fingers in an ovenproof dish and sprinkle them with the Marsala or brandy.

Whisk the egg whites until stiff and add the sugar, whisking until the mixture is glossy.

Take the vanilla ice cream out of the freezer and leave it to soften slightly.

Smooth the ice cream over the lady fingers or sponge-cakes.

Spread the meringue mixture over the ice cream until it is completely covered.

If preferred, sprinkle the whole thing with sliced almonds and immediately place in the preheated oven for 20 minutes, or until the meringue mixture is lightly brown.

Serve immediately.

A great combination of cold and hot, this dessert will transport you to those snowy peaks.

black forest chocolate roulade

serves 6

1 lb canned pitted black
    cherries in syrup, drained
kirsch or cherry brandy
6 oz bittersweet or semisweet
    chocolate (the higher percentage
    of cocoa solids, the better)

5 large eggs, separated
1 cup sugar
2 cups heavy cream or non-dairy
    cream, whisked
confectioner's sugar

The night before making the roulade, place the drained cherries in a bowl covered with your chosen liqueur and refrigerate.

Preheat the oven to 350°F.

Melt the chocolate by putting it in a glass bowl over a saucepan filled with hot water.

Put the egg yolks and sugar in a mixing bowl and beat until pale. Add the melted chocolate. Beat until the mixture is smooth. Whisk the egg whites and fold into the mixture.

Pour into a jelly-roll pan lined with parchment paper that overlaps the sides. Bake in the preheated oven for 15 to 20 minutes. Take out of the oven and leave to cool. Turn out onto waxed paper that has been dusted with confectioner's sugar.

Whisk the cream and spread over the roulade. Drain the cherries, reserving the liqueur. With a hand blender, purée the cherries, then spread the purée over the cream.

Roll up the roulade; use the waxed paper, which is underneath, to help you. Place on a serving dish and decorate with confectioner's sugar. Pour the reserved cherry liqueur in a jug to use when serving.

The seventies' dish reinvented. Very retro!

bread-and-butter pudding

serves 6

soft, unsalted butter
orange marmalade
16 slices thick white bread,
   crusts removed
1/4 cup sultanas
   (golden or white raisins)

3 large eggs
1 1/4 cups milk
1 1/4 cups whipping cream
3/4 cup sugar
grated rind of 1 orange
1 tablespoon light brown sugar

Preheat the oven to 350°F.

Grease a 10-inch ovenproof dish.

Spread the butter and marmalade on the bread and make a sandwich. Then butter the top of each sandwich.

After you have done all your sandwiches, cut them in two diagonally to create triangles.

Layer the triangles in the dish. Sprinkle on the sultanas.

In a separate bowl, whisk together the eggs, milk, cream, and sugar. Pour over the triangles.

Grate the rind of the orange over the top and sprinkle on the brown sugar.

Put the ovenproof dish inside a large roasting pan half-filled with water and place in the middle of the preheated oven. Bake for 30 minutes.

This should be served hot with cream or real egg custard—fantastic as a real carb blowout!

caramel ice cream

serves 6

½ cup granulated sugar
4 large egg yolks

2½ cups non-dairy cream

In a saucepan, combine the sugar with four tablespoons of water and stir over a moderate heat until the sugar has dissolved completely. Let the sugar boil, swirling the pan occasionally until the sugar turns a light-brown color.

Pour eight tablespoons of water into the caramel and simmer, stirring until it has melted.

Beat the egg yolks. Pour the syrup into them and continue beating until the mixture thickens.

Whisk the cream and fold it into the mixture.

Pour the ice cream into a freezer-proof container and place in the freezer to set.

Try freezing the ice cream in a kugelhopf or bundt pan. When you turn it out, you'll have a hole in the middle, which you can then fill with various fruits.

cheater's cheese blintzes

serves 12

for the pancakes
(to cheat even more,
   just buy some ready-made!)
2 cups all-purpose flour
2 large eggs
2 ⅓ cups whole milk
grated rind of 1 lemon
4 tablespoons oil, for frying

¼ cup unsalted butter, to brush
   over the blintzes

for the filling
1 lb cream cheese (I use light)
⅓ cup sour cream
2 large egg yolks
3 tablespoons sugar
1 teaspoon vanilla extract
a generous ⅓ cup sultanas
   (golden or white raisins)
pinch of salt

to serve
sour cream, cherry jam or
   apple sauce

Mix all the pancake ingredients, except the oil, in a blender
and refrigerate for at least half an hour, or even better, overnight.
When the above mixture is ready, make the filling simply by
mixing together all the filling ingredients.

Whisk the batter before using to ensure a good consistency; you
can easily do this with a hand whisk.

Coat an 8-inch round, thin frying pan by pouring the oil onto it
and swirling it around the pan, then pouring out any excess and
wiping around the pan with a paper towel.

Heat the coated frying pan and pour on a thin layer of batter.

The pancake is ready when the mixture starts to bubble or comes away from the sides, so when that happens, just flip it over to brown it lightly. The first pancake is always a disaster, so don't worry—just eat it!

Turn the pancakes out onto a baking or cookie sheet. Continue this method, but keep oiling the pan after every two pancakes. Just stack the pancakes one on top of the other and leave to cool.

You should make approximately a dozen.

the blintz
Preheat the oven to 375°F.

Take one pancake and fill it with the mixture, roll up the pancake, fold its sides and place in an ovenproof dish. Continue to do so with the others until the dish is filled.

Melt 2oz unsalted butter and brush over the blintzes.

Bake in the preheated oven for 20 minutes, or until lightly browned.

Blintzes are delicious served warm with sour cream, cherry jam or apple sauce—or all three if you desire! If you're in a rush, just buy ready-made pancakes; they work equally well.

choca-challah pudding

serves 6

unsalted butter, for greasing
8 slices of a large *challah*
⅝-inch thick (one day old)
½ lb bittersweet or semisweet
chocolate (the higher percentage
of cocoa solids, the better)
1 cup heavy cream

1¼ cups skimmed milk
½ cup unsalted butter
1 scant cup sugar
4 medium eggs

for decoration
confectioner's sugar

Butter a medium ovenproof dish (I always use an oval one that's 14in x 9½in x 2½in).

Remove the crusts from the *challah*. If the slices are very large, cut them in half.

Place the chocolate, cream, milk, butter, and sugar into a double boiler (bain-marie) over a low heat, stirring all the time, until the mixture is melted and smooth. If you haven't got a double boiler, then just use a saucepan of boiling water with a heatproof bowl over it and put the ingredients in the bowl.

Remove the bowl from the heat and leave it to cool.

Beat the eggs and stir them slowly into the chocolate mixture.

Pour half the sauce into the bottom of the ovenproof dish.

Place the sliced *challah* into the liquid, pressing down with the back of a tablespoon to allow the bread to begin to saturate.

Pour the remaining liquid on top and press down again to allow the sauce to saturate the bread and completely cover the *challah*.

Cover the dish and leave to cool, then refrigerate it for a minimum of two hours.

Preheat the oven to 350°F.

Bake in a bain-marie (I do this by putting the dish in a roasting pan and filling it with water until it reaches halfway up the outside of the dish) in the preheated oven for about 20 minutes.

Dust with with confectioner's sugar to decorate and serve warm.

A fantastic way of using leftover challah—and a wonderfully chocolicious dessert.

coffee and amaretti ice

serves 8

3 large eggs
⅓ cup sugar
1¼ cups non-dairy cream

3 tablespoons coffee extract
¼ lb amaretti cookies

Whisk the eggs and sugar together until pale and creamy in color, with a texture like whipped cream.

Add the non-dairy cream to the mixture and continue to whisk until thick.

Whisk in the coffee extract.

Bash the cookies with a rolling pin to form broken pieces and fold these into the mixture.

Place the mixture into a container and freeze overnight.

A gondola moment.

fruit brûlée

serves 6

seasonal fruit such as
   strawberries, raspberries or
   fresh peaches
2½ cups heavy cream

1 vanilla bean, split
4 large egg yolks
1 level tablespoon sugar
extra sugar, for the caramel

Make a fruit salad in advance and put it into an ovenproof dish.

To make the brûlée, put the cream and the vanilla bean into a
double boiler (bain-marie) over a moderate heat. (If you haven't
got a double boiler, use a saucepan of boiling water with a
heatproof bowl over it and put the ingredients in the bowl.)
Stir continuously and bring to scalding point.

Beat the four egg yolks thoroughly with the sugar.

Remove the vanilla bean from the cream and pour in the egg-yolk
mixture. Turn down the heat and stir continuously for about five
minutes, until the cream thickens. Keep a very beady eye on this
tricky procedure; if the mixture boils, it will be ruined!

Pour this warm, thick mixture over the fruit salad. Cool. Place in the
refrigerator for at least six hours (or better still, overnight) to set.

The next day, cover the brûlée evenly with about ¼-inch of sugar
and place under a preheated very, very hot grill or broiler, turning
the dish to allow the mixture to melt in order to caramelize. Make
sure the top is evenly browned, then serve.

*For this procedure, you can use a chef's blowtorch—but watch
out for your nails!*

honey halva ice cream

serves 8

3 large eggs
⅓ cup sugar
1¼ cups non-dairy cream

½ lb *halva*—plain or any other
flavor of your choice, crumbled
2 tablespoons clear honey

Whisk the eggs and sugar until pale cream in color, with a texture like whipped cream.

Whisk the cream until thick and then fold the crumbled *halva* into the cream.

Fold the egg mixture gently into the cream mixture, then drizzle in the honey and fold it in gently.

Put the mixture into an ice-cream bombe container (or any container suitable for freezing) and leave overnight in the freezer.

For those who have a sweet tooth, grab a spoon and indulge!

A Jewish Princess knows that
being happy keeps you young,
so I suggest a fabulous anti-aging
cream. You can buy it everywhere,
it comes in huge pots, it's very
economical, and it's always
available when you're feeling
a little blue.

The name? Ice cream.
Just don't apply too much!

meringue malibu roulade

serves 6

5 large egg whites
1½ cups superfine sugar
¼ lb shredded coconut
confectioner's sugar, for dusting

1 cup whisked non-dairy cream
   (or the real mccoy)
1 tablespoon Malibu coconut rum
½ lb chopped pineapple

Preheat the oven to 325°F.

Whisk the egg whites until stiff, then add the superfine sugar. Whisk until the mixture forms thick peaks.

Fold in the shredded coconut.

Line a jelly-roll pan with parchment paper.

Spoon the mixture onto the parchment paper and spread it evenly with a spatula. Bake in the preheated oven for 30 minutes.

Cover with a clean, damp dishcloth and leave to cool for at least two hours; the dishcloth keeps the cake from drying out.

Place a large sheet of parchment paper on a kitchen surface and dust it with the confectioner's sugar.

Whisk the cream with the Malibu.

Turn the roulade onto the parchment paper and spread it with the Malibu cream.

Place the pineapple chunks all over the cream.

Take the ends of parchment paper and start to roll. DO THIS ALONE SO YOU DON'T FEEL PRESSURED!

Place the roulade into an oblong dish and decorate with any leftover pineapple.

If cracks appear, don't worry—that's how it's supposed to look! This is a surprisingly sophisticated desert, but easy to do and well worth the effort.

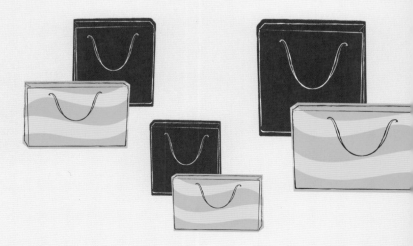

pecan pie

serves 6

½ lb medium-flake pastry (or buy
  a ready-made frozen piecrust
  if you want to save time!)
3 large eggs
¾ cup golden syrup
  (if unavailable, use equal parts
  honey and light corn syrup)

1 tablespoon grand marnier
pinch of salt
½ cup (packed) light brown sugar
½ lb pecans, shelled

Preheat the oven to 350°F.

Line a 9-inch pie plate with the pastry.

Fill with "baking beans" (or—cover with parchment paper, and fill
with ordinary beans or rice), then bake in the oven for 10 minutes.

Leave to cool and remove the beans.

Cream together the eggs, golden syrup, and Grand Marnier.

Add the pinch of salt and brown sugar and mix well.

Fold in the pecans.

Pour the mixture into the piecrust and bake for 20 minutes,
or until the filling has risen and turned light brown.

Serve warm or cold.

For extra calories, add a spoonful of vanilla ice cream.

shikerer's tipple

serves 6

½ gallon vanilla ice cream
1 lb dried pitted
  prunes, chopped
¾ cup sultanas
  (golden or white raisins)

1 cup brandy
4 oz (approximately ⅔ cup)
  semisweet chocolate chips

Soak the prunes and sultanas in the brandy for an hour.

Take the ice cream out of the freezer and allow it to thaw slightly.

Place the ice cream, prunes, sultanas, and brandy into a mixer and blend well.

Stir in the chocolate chips.

Pour the ice-cream mixture into a freezer-proof serving dish and place in freezer to set.

This is a great accompaniment to any dessert or pie.

sticky briti pudding

serves 6-8

2 15 oz cans of pears, in juice
  (reserve 1 can of juice)
1/4 cup unsalted butter
1 1/3 cups (unpacked) dark
  brown sugar
2 large eggs
2 cups self-rising flour
1/2 cup dark rum
1 teaspoon baking soda

for the sauce
1 1/4 cups heavy cream
1 1/3 cups (unpacked) dark
  brown sugar
1/3 cup unsalted butter

Preheat the oven to 350°F.

Butter an 8-inch ovenproof dish. Arrange one can's worth of drained sliced pears on the bottom of dish.

In a large bowl, mix together the butter, sugar, eggs, and flour.

Put the other can of drained pears, the rum, and 4 fl oz (1/2 cup) of pear juice in a saucepan and simmer for 4 minutes.

Remove from the heat and allow to cool.

Stir in the baking soda.

Add the pear mixture to the butter mixture, then pour into the ovenproof dish and bake for 30–40 minutes in the preheated oven.

Check that the pudding is cooked through by putting a knife in the middle; if it comes out clean, it's done.

To make the sauce, mix all the sauce ingredients in the saucepan and cook gently until the sugar has dissolved.

Make a few holes in the pudding with a knife or other sharp instrument.

Pour the sauce onto the pudding, allowing it to seep through, and serve.

You can double the mixture and freeze one for a later date. Alternatively, put the pudding in the freezer and defrost when ready to use. You can then make the sauce while reheating the pudding, which will take 20 minutes in a hot oven. Then just pour on the sauce as described above.

summer fruit pavlova

serves 8

the whites of 4 large eggs
1½ cups superfine sugar
1 cup heavy cream
   (or non-dairy version)

4 kiwi fruits, for decorating
   (or any other fruit in season)

Preheat the oven to 275°F.

Make a pattern by drawing a soft pencil line around a large round plate on a baking or cookie sheet.

Whisk the egg whites until stiff and add the superfine sugar slowly while still whisking. Continue whisking until the mixture forms stiff peaks.

Use a spatula and shape the mixture onto the circle on the baking or cookie sheet to form a round pavlova.

Bake in the preheated oven for about one and a half hours, then switch off the heat and leave the pavlova to cool inside the oven—the longer, the better.

When ready to serve, whisk the cream and spread it over the pavlova, and decorate with the fruits of your choice.

You can change the fruits according to the season—a bit like your clothes.

ten-minute trifle

serves 8

2 raspberry jelly rolls
1 small bowl filled with sherry
2 15 oz cans of raspberries, in
    heavy syrup, drained
2 large handfuls of roasted
    sliced almonds
1 1/4 cups fresh, sweet raspberries

2 cups fresh, thick egg custard
1 1/4 cups heavy cream
*all of the above ingredients are
    approximate—it really depends
    on the size of the bowl you are
    going to use*

Slice the jelly rolls and dip the pieces into the bowl of sherry until
the cake is saturated.

Line the bottom and sides of a glass dish with the jelly rolls.

Pour on the drained raspberries and half of the almonds.

Next, add the fresh raspberries.

Pour the custard over the fruit.

Refrigerate.

Whisk the cream..

Dry pan-fry the rest of the almonds until golden.

Spread the cream on top of the trifle and sprinkle with the
toasted almonds.

*This may take only ten minutes to make, but your guests will
be impressed.*

tiramisu

serves 6

4 large eggs, separated
1 cup sugar
1 lb mascarpone cheese
   (approximately 2¼ cups)
2 boxes lady fingers
   (approximately 44)

approximately 1¼ cups marsala
approximately 2 tablespoons
   coffee extract
cocoa powder

Beat together the egg yolks and sugar, then add the cheese and beat until it forms a smooth, creamy mixture.

Whisk the egg whites until soft peaks form.

Slowly whisk the egg whites into the cheese mixture.

In a shallow bowl, pour in the wine and coffee extract.

Quickly dip the lady fingers, one at a time, into the wine mixture and place at the bottom of a glass dish about 13 in x 9 in.

Place the lady fingers next to each other to form a line of a single layer.

Pour a layer of the cheese mixture over these, then place another layer of quickly dipped lady fingers over the cheese mixture, and finally pour on the remaining cheese mixture.

Sift the cocoa powder over the top of the dessert and put it in the refrigerator to set.

The Jewish version of the Italian mama's cheesecake.

A waiter came to take the
table's dessert order.
The Jewish Princess wanted a
little of everything—so when
her turn came, she knew exactly
what to request:

"A fork, please!"

toffee apple pie

serves 8

for the base
1/3 cup melted unsalted butter
1/2 lb graham crackers, crushed
  (put them in a bag and bash
  them with a rolling pin)

for the toffee
1 3/4 cups condensed milk
1/3 cup sugar
1/4 cup unsalted butter

for the filling
3/4 lb (about 2–3 medium) eating
  apples, peeled and quartered
1 tablespoon maple syrup

for the topping
1 1/4 cups heavy cream,
  lightly whipped
semisweet or milk chocolate,
  for decoration

Mix the melted butter with the crushed graham crackers.

Press into the base of an 8.5-inch springform pan and chill for ten minutes.

Put the condensed milk, sugar, and butter in a nonstick saucepan. Place the saucepan over a low heat, stirring constantly.

Once the butter has melted, increase the heat and bring the mixture up to boiling point, stirring constantly and lifting the saucepan off the heat to stop the sauce from burning. The mixture will thicken; this should take no longer than five minutes.

Pour the mixture over the base and return it to the fridge.

Place the apple pieces in a microwavable dish.

Cook on a high heat in the microwave for six minutes.

Halfway through, remove the dish from the microwave, stir the apples, and then replace to ensure even cooking.

Drain and mix with the maple syrup.

Place the syrupy apples on top of the toffee and put the pie back in the fridge.

Whisk the cream and spread it on top of the pie, then decorate with shavings of milk or semisweet chocolate.

To ensure that the toffee apple pie stays in one piece, use a sharp knife and run it around the edge of the pan before removing it.

8

cakes

cakes just like grandma made

My grandmother made unbelievable cakes. Her cakes were actually legendary, and to this day my friends still reminisce about the after-school tea parties we had.

Whenever she used to visit, she always arrived with trays and trays of farm-laid eggs, crates and crates of fruit, and other bulk purchases from the discount store. I think this bulk-buying habit was due to the war years and her fear of not having enough food. My mother and I seem to have followed suit and are always overstocking our refrigerators and freezers ("just in case").

Grandma would spend her visits glued to the food mixer in the kitchen, baking and baking—and of course I liked nothing better than to spend time with her: helping, licking the bowl, watching, and sniffing the delicious aroma of *cake*.

I have to confess that I was a bit of a loser in my early teens; yes, even Jewish Princesses can have some "backward" years! My social life was practically zero. While my friends had boyfriends and were partying their nights away, my family had moved—and we were, as far as I was concerned, too far from civilization. My Saturday nights were spent, I'm almost ashamed to say, *baking*.

I realize now, however, just how incredibly therapeutic baking is. I am sure my grandma used to bake so much to get over the loss of my beloved grandpa. I, in turn, baked so much to cope with yearning for my knight in shining armor to turn up on his white charger. Amazingly, he eventually did turn up: not "on," but "in" a white Honda Prelude—nearly Princess Perfect!

So forget yoga or Pilates; baking is an incredible way to escape your troubles and get lost in a world of flour, eggs, and sugar. To see such basic ingredients transformed into treats as wonderful as the cakes in this chapter is always a truly satisfying experience.

almond cake

1 cup softened unsalted butter
1 cup sugar
4 medium eggs, separated
1 pinch of salt
1 1/3 cups self-rising flour
2 oz ground almonds
1 teaspoon baking powder
1 teaspoon almond extract

for the icing
approximately 2 tablespoons
   boiling water
1 3/4 cups confectioner's sugar
1/3 cup sliced almonds

Preheat the oven to 325°F.

Cream the butter and sugar until pale.

In another bowl, whisk the egg whites until they form soft peaks (add a pinch of salt).

Mix the self-rising flour with the ground almonds and baking powder.

Add the dry ingredients to the creamed butter and sugar.

Slowly add the egg yolks and almond extract.

Fold in the egg whites.

Line or grease a 8.5-inch springform pan.

Pour in the mixture and bake in the preheated oven for 35 to 40 minutes.

Cool before turning out onto a wire rack.

To make the icing, slowly stir the boiling water into the confectioner's sugar.

Place the icing in a double boiler (bain-marie) over a low heat, and keep stirring until the sugar has melted and the icing is easy to spread. (If you don't have a bain-marie, place the ingredients in a bowl and put this over a pan of boiling water.)

Heat a frying pan and dry-fry the sliced almonds.

Once you've iced the cake, decorate it with the toasted almonds.

Don't feel too guilty when eating this treat, as almonds are great for the skin!

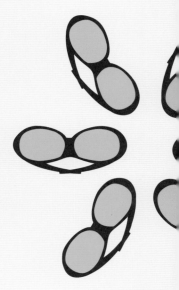

anytime cake

1 cup unsalted butter
1 1/2 cups sugar
4 medium eggs
1 teaspoon vanilla extract
2 level cups self-rising flour

optional extras
3/4 cup sultanas (golden or
    white raisins)
or 4 oz (about 2/3 cup)
    chocolate chips
or 4 oz (about 1/2 cup) glacé
    (candied) cherries...or all three!

Preheat the oven to 350°F.

Cream the butter and sugar, then add the rest of the ingredients—
and then add an optional extra to make it into the cake you
decide to break your diet for!

Pour the batter into a greased 8-inch baking pan.

Bake in the preheated oven for 45 minutes to an hour, testing
with a knife to see if it has cooked through.

*The cake mixture can also be divided into muffin tins.
Bake them for ten minutes, then decorate with confectioner's
sugar and sprinkles to make children's cupcakes.*

apple brûlée cake

3 medium eating apples, peeled and thinly sliced
1 level cup self-rising flour
1 teaspoon baking powder
¾ cup sugar
⅓ cup milk
4 tablespoons unsalted butter, melted

2 medium eggs
1 teaspoon cinnamon

for the topping
⅓ cup unsalted butter, softened
¾ cup superfine sugar
1 teaspoon vanilla extract
1 egg

Preheat the oven to 325°F.

Put the thinly sliced apples into the base of a greased and floured 8.5-inch springform pan.

Put the rest of the cake ingredients into a bowl and beat until smooth.

Pour the batter over the apples, spreading it evenly, and bake in the preheated oven for 30 to 40 minutes, or until lightly golden.

Meanwhile, cream together the topping ingredients.

Remove the cake from the oven and spoon over the topping.

Bake for a further 20 to 25 minutes, until the topping is a golden brown.

This cake is delicious served hot or cold. The way to my husband's heart is with this cake—but he's taken!

as sweet as channie "honey" cake

3²/₃ cups self-rising flour
1½ cups sugar
grated rind and juice of
   1 large orange
1 teaspoon allspice
1 teaspoon cinnamon
½ teaspoon baking soda

1 cup corn oil
3 medium eggs
1⅓ cups golden syrup
   (if unavailable, use ²/₃ cup each
   honey and light corn syrup)
1 cup boiled water
sliced almonds, for decorating

Preheat the oven to 350°F.

Sift the flour.

In a bowl, mix all dry ingredients together—*i.e.* flour, sugar, orange rind, allspice, cinnamon, and baking soda.

Combine all the wet ingredients in another bowl, then add them to the dry ingredients. Mix together.

Pour the mixture into a 10-inch square cake pan and decorate with sliced almonds if desired.

Bake in the preheated oven for 50 to 60 minutes, always checking towards the end.

Even though there is no honey in this cake when it's made with golden syrup, it is still considered "honey" cake by JPs. Honey cake is always made for the Jewish New Year to wish friends and family sweet success for the coming year. This one is delicious served warm, sliced, and buttered.

banana cake

1 cup softened unsalted butter
1⅔ cups sugar
2 large egg yolks
2 level cups all-purpose flour
1 teaspoon baking powder

½ teaspoon salt
4 tablespoons sour cream
2 medium-sized ripe bananas
1 teaspoon vanilla extract
5 large egg whites, whisked

Preheat the oven to 350°F.

Mix the butter and sugar together.

Add the egg yolks to the mixture and continue to beat.

Add the flour, baking powder, salt, sour cream, bananas, and vanilla and blend well.

Fold in the whisked egg whites.

Pour the batter into a greased 8-inch square pan and bake in the preheated oven for 45 minutes.

This is great served warm with butter. Even if people don't like bananas, they will be surprised at how delicious this recipe is.

a word about cheesecake

There are many reasons why I love making cheesecake.

1   It's a fantastic stress release when you bash the hell out of those graham crackers (are your children getting on your nerves?), plus it's a pretty good arm workout.

2   It usually qualifies for the fewer-than-ten-ingredients rule.

3   It always comes out of the oven completely level, so it looks highly professional.

4   It takes ten minutes to prepare and 30 minutes to cook so I can still go to my Sunday spinning class.

5   What really encouraged me in my baking of cheesecake was when I gave a cheesecake to one of my husband's clients (very, very famous artists) and they said (just wait for this—it's very exciting and great for my Princess ego) that it was: "The BEST cheesecake they had ever tasted."

Do you think if I made them enough cheesecake they would give me a "piece" of their work?

Every Jewish Princess knows
that cakes have no calories if you:
* take a bite from somebody
   else's plate;
* stand on one leg when eating;
* sniff them;
* only eat the top;
* only eat the bottom;
* only ever nibble a sliver!

If you're suffering with PMT
(Princess Menstrual Tension),
of course, then anything goes!

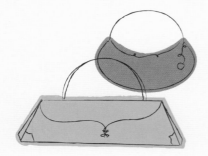

peanut butter cheesecake

8 graham crackers
2 tablespoons smooth
   peanut butter
1 tablespoon unsalted butter
1 cup sugar
4 medium eggs
1 lb cream cheese (regular or lite)
2 tablespoons sour cream

peanut butter topping
3 tablespoons smooth
   peanut butter
2 tablespoons sour cream
1 tablespoon light cream
superfine sugar to taste
a handful of crushed
   salted peanuts

Preheat the oven to 300°F.

Crush the graham crackers by putting them into a bag and bashing them with a rolling pin.

In a small saucepan, melt the peanut butter and butter, then add the crushed graham crackers and mix well.

In a greased, round springform pan, approximately 8 inches in diameter, press the graham cracker mixture down to form the base.

Beat together the sugar and eggs until the mixture is light and frothy.

Add the cream cheese and sour cream.

Cook for approximately 20 minutes in the preheated oven, or until the edges are firm but the middle is slightly wobbly.

Turn off the oven and let the cake cool inside with the door slightly open.

When cold, refrigerate it for at least two to three hours.

To make the topping, melt the peanut butter in a saucepan on a low heat, then add the sour cream and the light cream— DO NOT let the mixture boil!

As soon as these ingredients are stirred in, remove from the heat and add enough sugar to suit your own taste.

When the topping is cool, remove the cheesecake from the fridge and spread the peanut butter topping on top.

Garnish with a handful of crushed salted peanuts.

If you like peanut butter, this cheesecake is orgasmic!

the ultimate cheesecake

for the base
1 lb graham crackers, crushed
1 teaspoon cinnamon
½ cup melted
  unsalted butter
½ cup sugar

for the cake
approximately ⅔ cup sultanas
  (golden or white raisins)
2 large eggs
3 tablespoons milk
1¼ lb cream cheese
½ cup sugar
1 teaspoon vanilla extract

for the topping
1¼ cups sour cream
1 teaspoon
  vanilla extract
2 tablespoons sugar

for decoration
fresh fruit

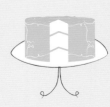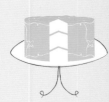

Preheat the oven to 350°F.

To make the base, mix together the base ingredients, making sure the graham crackers are well-crushed, and press into a 9–10-inch springform pan. Use a fork to press the mixture down on the base and up around the sides until the pan is well-covered.

Bake in the preheated oven for ten minutes.

Cool, then sprinkle the sultanas over the bottom.

Mix together the rest of the ingredients, pour on top of the base, and bake for 30 minutes.

Remove the cheesecake from the oven and allow it to cool for 15 minutes.

Meanwhile, make the topping by mixing all the topping ingredients together.

Pour over the cheesecake, return it to the oven and bake for a further ten minutes. Leave to cool.

Refrigerate overnight.

Pile fresh fruit such as strawberries and blueberries on top of this cheesecake. It gives it a great look and tastes delicious.

carrot cake

1 level cup self-rising flour
1 teaspoon baking powder
½ teaspoon cinnamon
1 pinch of salt
1⅓ cups light brown
  sugar (unpacked)
1 tablespoon olive oil
2 medium eggs
½ lb carrots, grated
1⅔ cups ground almonds

for the frosting
6 oz (about ¾ cup) light
  cream cheese
½ cup confectioner's sugar
2 tablespoons softened
  unsalted butter

for decoration
a handful of toasted pine nuts
  (optional)

Preheat the oven to 325°F.

Sift and mix together the flour, baking powder, cinnamon, and salt.

Add the brown sugar, olive oil, and eggs and mix well.

Mix in the carrots and ground almonds.

Put the mixture into a greased 8-inch cake pan and bake in the preheated oven for 30 minutes.

Turn the cake out onto a wire rack and leave it to cool.

To make the frosting, use a hand blender to mix all ingredients together in a bowl until smooth.

When the cake is cold, spread the frosting on top.

Decorate with toasted pine nuts, if desired.

A cake full of vitamins that can be used to improve your suntan if eaten regularly!

chocolate refrigerator cake

½ lb bittersweet or
  semisweet chocolate
2 large eggs
4 teaspoons sugar
1 cup melted unsalted butter
½ lb graham crackers, crushed
²/₃ cups salted peanuts

³/₄ cups chopped walnuts
½ lb glacé (candied)
  cherries, chopped
1 teaspoon vanilla extract
a handful of walnut halves,
  for decoration

Break the chocolate into squares and place in a double boiler (bain-marie) or in a small bowl over a pan of hot water to melt.

Beat the eggs and sugar together, then beat in the melted butter.

Stir in the chocolate and fold in the broken graham crackers, together with the nuts, cherries, and vanilla extract.

Pour the mixture into a buttered Pyrex dish 6–7 inches deep and leave in the fridge to set for at least six hours.

When ready to turn out, use a sharp knife and run it around the edges of the cake. Immerse the dish halfway in hot water to allow the cake to melt a bit and then turn it out.

Decorate with the walnuts and refrigerate until ready to use.

When serving, cut into small slices—this cake is very rich. Delicious used as a petit four with coffee.

deluxe chocolate cake

6 oz bittersweet or semisweet
   chocolate (the higher percentage
   of cocoa solids, the better)
1/2 cup softened unsalted butter
1 tablespoon grand marnier
5 medium eggs, separated
1 1/3 cups ground almonds
1 pinch of salt

1/2 cup sugar
2 tablespoons heavy cream

for the raspberry glaze
4 tablespoons raspberry jam
1 tablespoon sugar

Preheat the oven to 325°F.

Melt the chocolate and butter in a double boiler (bain-marie), stirring constantly so that the mixture does not burn. If you don't have a double boiler, then just use a saucepan of boiling water with a heatproof bowl over it and put the ingredients in the bowl.

Let the chocolate mixture cool. You can speed this up by standing the bowl in cold water.

Stir in the Grand Marnier, egg yolks, and ground almonds.

In a separate bowl, whisk the egg whites with a pinch of salt until soft peaks form, then slowly add the sugar.

Gently fold the egg whites into the chocolate mixture.

Add the cream and gently fold it into the mixture.

Pour into a greased and floured 8-inch springform pan.

Place in the center of the preheated oven for 25 minutes, or until a knife stuck in the middle comes out clean.

When the cake has cooled, remove it from the pan and place it on a serving dish.

When you are ready to glaze the cake, put the raspberry jam and sugar in a saucepan and heat gently, stirring so that the glaze does not burn. When the mixture becomes syrupy, remove it from the heat.

Pour the glaze over the top and let it run down the sides.

Even when this cake is served as a dessert after a large meal, there is never any left over! If you don't like raspberry jam, simply try making the glaze with the jam of your choice.

english fruitcake with a cup of tea

1⅓ cups mixed chopped
   dried fruit
grated rind of
   1 whole orange
4 english breakfast tea bags
2½ cups hot water
3 large eggs
¾ cup sugar
½ cup softened unsalted butter
2 tablespoons milk

2¼ cups self-rising flour,
   plus 3 tablespoons
1 teaspoon baking powder

for decoration
1 handful of blanched almonds
1 tablespoon light brown sugar

Preheat the oven to 300°F.

Place the dried fruit and orange rind in a large heatproof bowl.

Make a pot of tea with the four tea bags and boiling water and leave it to brew.

Pour the tea over the fruit until it is just covered and leave to marinate for a couple of hours.

Whisk the eggs and sugar together until the mixture has expanded and is nice and frothy.

Add the butter slowly, in small pieces.

Strain the fruit, reserving the tea, and dry it on paper towels, then lightly dust it with the three tablespoons of flour.

With the mixer set on slow, add the fruit, milk, and the reserved tea to the egg, sugar, and butter mixture.

Sift together the 2¼ cups self-rising flour and the baking powder, then add this to the cake mixture.

Grease and flour an 8-inch springform pan and pour in the batter.

Decorate with a handful of blanched almonds and brown sugar.

Bake in the preheated oven for 55 to 60 minutes.

A very useful after-school cake. This is at its best made the day before serving.

grandpa's favorite coffee and walnut cake

1 cup unsalted butter
1½ cups sugar
4 large eggs
1 cup chopped walnuts
2 tablespoons coffee extract
2 level cups self-rising flour
2 teaspoons baking powder

for the icing
¾ cup unsalted butter
3½ cups confectioner's
  sugar, sifted
4 tablespoons milk
2 tablespoons coffee extract

for decoration
walnut halves and coffee beans

Preheat the oven to 325°F.

Mix all the cake ingredients together and divide the mixture into two greased 7-inch baking pans.

Bake in the preheated oven for 25 to 30 minutes, checking that the cakes are baked by putting a skewer in. If it comes out clean, they're done.

Remove the cakes from the oven and leave them to cool.

Make the icing by combining all the ingredients, then use some of it to sandwich the cakes together.

Ice the cake all over, and decorate with walnut pieces interspersed with coffee beans.

The best present for Grandpa on birthdays, anniversaries or any occasion.

honey cake

2 level cups all-purpose flour
³/₄ cup sugar
1 teaspoon cinnamon
1 teaspoon allspice
3 tablespoons clear honey
⅓ cup golden syrup (if
  unavailable, use 3 tablespoons
  each honey and light corn syrup)

¼ cup cooking oil
2 medium eggs
1 teaspoon baking soda
about ⅓ cup smooth orange juice

Preheat the oven to 325°F.

Grease and flour an 8-inch cake pan.

In a large bowl, mix together the flour, sugar, and spices.

Add the honey, syrup, oil, and eggs.

Beat well until smooth.

Use another large bowl and dissolve the baking soda in the orange juice. Stir well (this will fizz) and then add this to the mixture.

Bake in the preheated oven for 40 to 50 minutes.

*It is a good idea to make this cake the day before eating.
As it matures, it becomes even more syrupy and delicious.*

marble cake

3 large eggs, separated
¾ cup unsalted butter
1½ cups sugar
1 teaspoon vanilla extract
2 level cups self-rising flour
3 tablespoons milk

3 oz (about ½ cup) semi-sweet
   chocolate chips (or milk
   chocolate, if you prefer)
4 tablespoons chocolate
   spread (or milk chocolate,
   if you prefer)

Preheat the oven to 350°F.

Whisk the egg whites until stiff. Leave them in the bowl and set aside for later.

In a separate bowl, beat the egg yolks, vanilla extract, and butter until creamy. Add the sugar gradually, beating until the mixture resembles whipped cream.

Now comes the tricky part. Keep the mixer going on low and add to it a tablespoon of flour; alternate with a tablespoon of milk and a tablespoon of the egg whites that you whisked at the beginning. Keep doing this until all the ingredients have been used. (This may be a pain, but it really is worth doing because it makes the cake very light.)

Divide the mixture in two. Place one half into a new bowl and add the chocolate drops to it.

Pour the mixture containing the chocolate drops into a greased 8-inch baking pan and spread it out over the bottom.

Add the chocolate spread to the other half of the mixture and mix well. Pour this over the chocolate-drop mixture in the baking pan.

By making a figure-eight with a spatula, swirl the dark chocolate-spread mixture gently through the chocolate-drop mixture, so that you get a marbling effect. When you do this, lift the spatula upwards to allow the white mixture to come to the top.

Smooth the top of the mixture and bake for 45 to 60 minutes.

I can remember fighting with my brother about whose turn it was to lick the bowl when we were children. Sometimes for children (and even a few adults!), this cake mixture is even more delicious than the finished cake. So leave the bowl for the kids—or if they're at school, add dishwashing liquid and quickly fill it with water; this will stop you from licking the bowl!

marmalade cream cake

¾ cup softened unsalted butter,
cut into small pieces
1 cup sugar
3 medium eggs
1 teaspoon
orange-flower water
3 tablespoons whole milk
1 tablespoon warm water
1¼ cups self-rising cake flour
2 teaspoons baking powder

for the marmalade-cream filling
1¼ cups whipping cream
3 tablespoons orange
marmalade ("thin-cut"—*i.e.* with
finely shredded peel)

for decoration
confectioner's sugar
grated rind of 1 whole orange

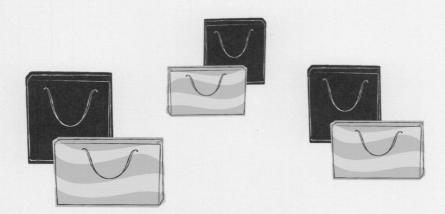

Preheat the oven to 325°F.

Grease and flour two 8-inch cake pans.

In a large bowl, cream the butter and sugar together until pale.

Add the eggs, one at a time, beating after each addition.

Add the orange-flower water and beat it in.

Mix the milk with the warm water, then add to the mixture and continue to beat.

Add all the dry ingredients and mix thoroughly.

Pour into the prepared cake pans and bake in the preheated oven for approximately 20 minutes.

Once the cakes have cooled, turn them out onto a wire rack.

To make the filling, whisk the whipping cream until firm.

Stir the marmalade so that it is loosened and soft, then add it gently to the whipped cream.

Use the marmalade cream to sandwhich the cakes together.

To decorate, grate the orange over the top of the cake and then lightly dust with confectioner's sugar.

This is a wonderful cake to serve on Sunday afternoons.

sour cream cake

⅓ cup unsalted butter
1 teaspoon cinnamon
6 oz (about 2 cups)
  graham crackers, crushed
1¾ cups sour cream
¾ cup sugar

1 medium egg
4 oz (about ½ cup) canned
  raspberries, drained
fresh raspberries, for decoration
more sour cream, for serving

Preheat the oven to 300°F.

Grease an 8.5-inch springform cake pan.

Melt the butter in a saucepan over a gentle heat. Add the cinnamon, stir, then add the cinnamon-butter to the crushed cookies in a large bowl.

Press the mixture into the bottom of the pan to make a base.

Bake in the preheated oven for five minutes.

Whisk together the sour cream, sugar, and egg.

Add the well-drained canned raspberries.

Pour the sour cream mixture over the base and bake for 40 minutes, or until set.

Remove the cake from the oven. When cool, refrigerate it in the pan for at least an hour to allow it to set.

Remove the cake from the pan right before serving.

Decorate with fresh raspberries and serve with a little sour cream on the side.

Be warned: one slice is never enough!

whiskey cake

finely grated rind of
  1 large orange
4 tablespoons whiskey
6 oz (approximately 1 packed
  cup) sultanas (white or
  golden raisins)

¾ cup unsalted butter
1 cup sugar
3 large eggs
2 level cups self-rising flour

Soak the grated orange rind in the whiskey for at least an hour, then add the sultanas and soak for a further 45 minutes.

Preheat the oven to 350°F.

Grease and line an 8-inch round cake pan with parchment paper.

In a large bowl, cream together the butter and sugar until light in color, then add the eggs.

Fold in the flour.

Add the sultanas and whiskey mixture.

Pour the batter into the prepared pan and bake in the middle of the preheated oven for one hour.

Cool completely before turning out and serving.

When the nights are drawing in, a slice of this is great with a cup of coffee or tea.

zesty lemon cake

4 medium eggs
1½ cups sugar
1 cup softened unsalted butter
2 tablespoons milk
1½ teaspoons
  lemon extract
grated rind of
  1 whole lemon
2 level cups self-rising flour
1 teaspoon baking powder

for the lemon syrup
juice of 2 lemons
grated rind of
  1 lemon
grated rind of
  1 orange
⅓ cup water
1 cup sugar

Preheat the oven to 350°F.

In a large bowl, whisk the eggs with the sugar until the mixture is frothy and the sugar is fully dissolved.

Add the softened butter, slowly, in small pieces.

Add the milk and lemon extract.

In another bowl, mix the rind of one whole lemon with the flour and baking powder, then add this to the egg mixture.

Pour the mixture into a greased and floured 8-inch x 8-inch square springform pan.

Place the pan in the middle of the preheated oven and bake for 45 minutes.

To make the syrup, place all of the syrup ingredients in a saucepan.

Bring to boiling point and keep it there for at least three minutes, sitrring constantly, until the syrup turns a golden color.

As the cake comes out of the oven, prick it all over and pour the syrup over the top. It looks lovely with the mixture of lemon and orange rind.

When the cake is cool, lift it out of the pan.

This cake is a combination of sweet and sharp, chewy and spongy—and absolutely delicious!

9

the ultimate dinner

the ultimate friday
night dinner

Friday night: the Sabbath or *Shabbos*. The night the family sits down together to share a wonderful meal. This is the night when the house is filled with incredible smells of cooking. The smell of chicken soup permeates every room.

The table is laid with a crisp, white tablecloth. The *Shabbos* candles sit in their treasured silver candlesticks. The gleaming silver *kiddush* cup filled with *kiddush* wine is ready for the blessing, and two wonderful freshly baked *challas* sit side by side, covered with a beautifully embroidered cloth.

This is the night when we reconnect with our spiritual being and are thankful for the week and the Sabbath still to come. For Jews, the Friday night dinner is a bit like Christmas—except instead of having to make this feast once a year, we have the blessing of making it once a week! The Friday night dinner fantasy is one of Father returning home from work in plenty of time before sundown, bearing flowers for his beautiful wife. The children are in their best clothes, faces shining like little angels, while Mother makes the blessing over the candles, looking like she has taken a break from the film set of *Fiddler on the Roof*. The house is serene, the conversation around the table jovial, interesting, and happy.

Unfortunately, I have since discovered that the fantasy of the Sabbath meal is, of course, nothing like reality.

Reality is: Husband returns home from work very, very late and flowerless. Your teenager has to be pried off the phone and strapped into her seat at the table, while the younger children, stuck with tons of homework, are moody and tired from a long week of school. Mother is— well, of course being a JP, *she's* perfect! But as far as the conversation around the table goes, if you're not careful, it can wind up turning into World War III.

Over the years, I have found ways of dealing with Friday night dinners and ways of turning the reality into at least a little bit of the fantasy. Firstly, I always try to invite guests over. On the face of it, this seems insane, but like most things in my life, there is method in my madness. Even though I now have more work to do, there are many advantages. For one thing, my husband magically gets home on time (even if he shoots in just before the guests arrive)—and sometimes he's even bearing flowers.

The teenager looks respectable and manages to unglue the phone from her ear (even teenagers have a social conscience).

The younger children are excited that guests are coming over and even enjoy showing off by helping to clear the table.

Guests always lighten the atmosphere, too, so there are never any arguments around the table—plus they are actually *grateful* for my culinary delights. An additional bonus is that we invariably get invited back, so there's one less Friday night dinner for me to do.

I have also learned to prepare the Friday night dinner early. Chicken soup is cooked on Wednesday, the table is laid and desserts made on Thursday, and on Friday I only allow one hour to prepare the rest of the food.

One hour may seem a short amount of time to prepare this feast, but as I have learned, you can prepare the same amount of food in one hour that used to take you days. It's just a matter of self-belief—and making things simple.

If, one week, you are too tired or too busy to do the full works, either cheat (otherwise known as "buy in") and make it look like your own, or simply simplify. No one will think any more or any less of you, and nobody wants to be greeted by a growling, resentful Princess hostess.

I am sure you have questioned why we even do Friday night dinner, but as Topol from *Fiddler on the Roof* said, "Tradition! Tradition!"

The Jewish Princess has a long
list of things she has to prepare
in order to be ready for the
Sabbath: manicure, pedicure,
hair color and cut, facial
and, of course, medication—
I mean, *meditation!*

chopped liver

serves 8

3 lb onions, roughly chopped
  (you can use
  frozen ready-sliced)
4 tablespoons corn oil
1 lb beef liver

4 large hard-boiled eggs
  (reserve 1 for decoration)
3 slices brown bread,
  crusts removed
salt and black pepper to taste

Liver is the only meat you buy from a kosher butcher that you need to kosher yourself (with special koshering utensils: ask a kosher butcher for advice). To do this, wash the liver to remove any blood, cover it with coarse salt, broil under an open flame, then rinse it thoroughly.

In a large frying pan, fry the onions in the corn oil until they turn a dark brown. The browner the onions get without burning, the better the result.

Cut the liver into strips and add it to the fried onions. Cook very slowly until the liver is soft and brown all the way through. Add a little more oil if necessary.

When the onions and liver are fully cooked, add the rest of the ingredients and blend well. Add salt and pepper to taste, but be sure to mix the seasoning thoroughly into the mixture.

Place in a serving dish. Using a coarse (large-holed) grater, grate the reserved egg over the top to decorate, and refrigerate.

If this is not for you, try buying it at your local kosher butcher—but I bet it won't taste half as good as this!

egg and onion

serves 8

10 medium hard-boiled eggs
1 bunch of spring onions,
    finely sliced
olive oil

salt and black pepper to taste
1 avocado (optional)
salad leaves and chopped
    tomatoes, for serving

Using a coarse (large-holed) grater, grate the hard-boiled eggs and stir in the sliced spring onion.

Add enough olive oil to bind the mixture.

Add salt and pepper to taste.

For a different twist, add the avocado: peel it and mash it with a bit of lemon juice and mix it into the egg mixture.

Use an ice-cream scoop to make individual servings. Place each serving on a bed of lettuce leaves and chopped tomatoes.

a word about chicken soup

Of all the soups in the Jewish kosher diet, none is more well-known or well-loved than chicken soup. And with good reason: this soup is traditionally served on Friday nights as part of the *Shabbos* dinner, and it is *wonderful*.

Out of all the chicken soups I have ever tasted, however, no two taste the same. Even when a recipe is handed down from mother to daughter, it still does not taste the same.

This is the Mystery and Magic of chicken soup: every recipe has something unique to offer.

I love my own chicken soup because it is full of intense flavor, it is low-fat, and it takes very little time to prepare. In fact, I always make my soup on a Wednesday evening so that I can leave it overnight to cool; this seems to intensify the flavor. Refrigerate it on Thursday morning, then just reheat it for Friday night.

Another handy tip I've discovered concerns *lockshen:* place a heaped tablespoon of cooked *lockshen* into the bottom of each individual soup bowl. As you pour the soup in, the *lockshen* will heat through.

Once you've got used to making chicken soup (whether by following this or any other recipe), you'll probably want to experiment with using other root vegetables or herbs to make your own version of this delicious elixir.

chicken soup

serves 10

1 fowl, skinned and cut
  into 8 pieces
  *NOTE: A fowl is a female
  chicken that's a bit like a mother-
  in-law—e.g. a "tough old bird."
  It can be purchased from any
  kosher butcher (the fowl, not
  the mother-in-law!).*
1 bunch of celery hearts, washed
8 carrots, peeled and left whole
4 turnips, peeled and cut into
  large chunks

2 parsnips, peeled and cut
  into large chunks
1 rutabaga, peeled and cut
  into large chunks.
1 large onion, peeled
  and cut into large chunks.
2 tablespoons dried parsley
salt and black pepper
  to taste
1 tablespoon chicken-flavored
  soup mix to every 2½ cups
  water used

Clean the fowl, removing any excess fat and anything else that looks vaguely suspicious.

Place it in a very large *shissel* (cooking pot).

Add all the rest of the ingredients and cover with cold water.

Bring the soup to a boil. Because there is no skin on the fowl, YOU WILL NOT NEED TO STAND THERE FOR HOURS REMOVING THE SCUM—so this is a perfect recipe for Princesses.

Turn the heat down to low, cover the saucepan, and leave to simmer gently for at least five hours, or more. You can test when the soup is ready by using a fork—the chicken should be so soft that it should practically fall away from the bone, and the soup should be a deep golden color.

to serve

If you have made this in advance, then when you take the soup out of the fridge to serve, get rid of any fat that has risen to the surface by laying several sheets of paper towels on top of the soup. When you remove it, the fat will cling to the paper.

If you're not worrying about your carbs, it's traditional to serve this soup with matzo balls and egg noodles (*see* Matzo Balls, page 196). Egg noodles can be purchased in any kosher section of the supermarket or delicatessen, but if you cannot be bothered to *shlep* around, just add some cooked pasta of your choice.

Finally, if you are lucky enough to have the golden eggs (*see* page 81), here's how to cook them. First, wash the eggs and peel off the outer layer. When you're ready to serve your chicken soup, just pop the eggs in the soup (also the matzo balls and *chicklach; see* page 196–7) and bring it to boiling point. Let it boil for five minutes to ensure that the eggs are cooked through.

Ahhhhhhh: Jewish Princess penicillin!

matzo balls (knaidlach)

serves 10

7 large matzos
1 large onion, diced
1 tablespoon olive oil
3 large eggs

3 tablespoons fine matzo meal
2 teaspoons
   chicken-flavored seasoning
salt and pepper to taste

Break the matzos into small pieces and place them in a colander. Soak with water. Leave to drain.

Fry the onion in the olive oil until brown.

Place in a mixer the matzos, eggs, matzo meal, onions, chicken flavoring, and salt and pepper. Mix all the above until you can see the mixture binding together.

Bring a large saucepan of salted water to the boil.

Wet your hands, then take a teaspoon of the mixture and roll it into a ball.

Continue to make the rest of the balls and then place them in the boiling water for 20 minutes.

This is a great accompaniment to Chicken Soup (see page 194) and is a bit different to the usual knaidlach.

chicklach (kosher-style dim sum)

serves 10

1 lb ground chicken
2 medium eggs
approximately 1 generous cup
    medium matzo meal
6 tablespoons or about ⅓ cup
    chicken fat (use the fat that
    comes off the top of the chicken
    soup—*see* page 194) or dairy-
    free margarine, melted

½ teaspoon cinnamon
½ teaspoon ginger
1 teaspoon dried parsley
salt and pepper to taste

Mix all the ingredients together and leave the mixture in the fridge to firm up for 20 minutes.

Wet your hands and, using a teaspoon as a measure, form the mixture into small balls.

Fill a large saucepan with salted water and bring it to the boil.

Drop the *chicklach* into the water and simmer for 30 minutes.

Use a slotted spoon to remove the *chicklach* from the water and add them to your chicken soup when needed (*see* below).

This new recipe will become a must as an accompaniment to Chicken Soup (see page 194).

roast chicken

serves 6

1 roasting chicken
2 onions, peeled
black pepper
dried parsley or sage
olive oil

chicken seasoning powder or
  chicken stock powder
12 mushrooms, washed and
  cut into quarters
spring onions, chopped
soy sauce

Preheat the oven to 350°F.

Clean the chicken. Just before putting it into the oven, pour boiling water through the center of the chicken and over the top to make the skin crispy.

Place the chicken in a roasting pan. Place one of the onions inside the chicken's cavity, then season the chicken with black pepper and sprinkle the parsley over the top. Rub a little olive oil into the skin to work the seasoning and parsley into the chicken.

Pour cold water into the bottom of the roasting pan (about 24–28 fl oz/3–3½ cups, depending on the size of chicken) and add a good sprinkling of chicken seasoning or stock powder.

Add the other onion, sliced, and the mushrooms, then add the chopped spring onions into the water and a splash of soy sauce onto the chicken.

Cook in the preheated oven for one hour 30 minutes. Lovely!

This recipe should serve six, depending on the size of the chicken. Unless my Uncle Michael is one of the guests—then it serves one...

roast potatoes

serves *as many as you like!*

roasting potatoes (allow at least
 2 large potatoes per person)

2–3 tablespoons olive oil
sea salt

Preheat the oven to 350°F.

Peel the potatoes and slice them in half.

Take a roasting pan and pour two to three tablespoons of olive oil over the bottom.

On each half of the potatoes, use a sharp knife and make slits (about five) across the potato's width. The slits should be three-quarters of the way down the potato; this allows the olive oil and seasoning to penetrate.

Place the potatoes in the dish, flat-side down.

Sprinkle them with olive oil and sea salt.

Bake in the preheated oven for one and a half hours, turning halfway through.

This elevates the humble roast potato to new heights. Make sure you make plenty for seconds.

shredded red cabbage with apples and sultanas

serves 6

1 red cabbage
1 apple, grated
3/4 cup sultanas
   (golden or white raisins)

5 tablespoons sweetener or sugar
1 1/4 cups white-wine vinegar
3 3/4 cups water

Preheat the oven to 300°F.

Slice the cabbage into thin slivers and rinse with water.

Mix the cabbage with the apple, sultanas, and sweetener and put into an ovenproof dish approximately 12 inches square.

Cover the mixture with the vinegar and water, making sure there is enough liquid to cover it completely.

Cover the dish with foil and bake in the preheated oven for approximately three hours. Keep an eye on it, and stir it every half an hour.

Do this the day you're going to have a manicure, since your hands can go a little bit purple. Better still, wear gloves when chopping.

sweet potato and carrot purée

serves 8

4 large sweet potatoes
8 large carrots
1 tablespoon vegetable
   bouillon powder

salt and black pepper to taste
1 tablespoon non-dairy margarine
1 medium egg, beaten

Peel all the vegetables and cut into chunks. Place them all in a large saucepan.

Barely cover the vegetables with water and add the vegetable bouillon powder.

Bring to the boil and simmer for 40 minutes. Drain and then purée.

Preheat the oven to 350°F.

Add the seasoning, margarine, and egg.

Pour the mixture into an ovenproof dish.

Bake in the preheated oven for 20 minutes.

I always use a hand blender to do the purée; it saves on time and dishwashing!

apple strudel pie

serves 6

for the dough
3 ⅔ cups all-purpose flour
1 cup sugar
1 cup unsalted butter
   or non-dairy margarine
4 large egg yolks (reserve the
   whites for later)
2 tablespoons milk
   (or soy milk if you want to
   keep the dessert *parev*)
1 teaspoon baking powder

for the filling
6 apples, peeled and sliced
1 level cup minus 1 tablespoon
   confectioner's sugar
3 teaspoons cinnamon
3 oz chopped walnuts
2 tablespoons
   vanilla-flavored sugar

4 large egg whites
   (set aside for later)

Make the dough from all the dough ingredients by using your hands to knead properly on a flat surface until everything is well-combined. If you don't want to get too sticky, mix the ingredients in your food mixer or processor. Cover the egg whites and place them in the fridge for use later.

Wrap a third of the dough in plastic wrap and place it in the freezer for at least an hour, until it is completely frozen and hard.

Wrap the remaining dough in plastic wrap and place it in the fridge.

When ready to proceed, preheat the oven to 350°F.

Whisk the egg whites until stiff. Set aside.

Place the rest of the ingredients in a large bowl and stir to make sure there is an even distribution of the sugars and cinnamon.

Roll out the dough from the fridge to whatever thickness works to cover the bottom and sides of the greased ovenproof pan you're using (I always use a 13-inch by 9-inch one).

Place the filling on top and spread the egg whites over the filling. Take out the dough from the freezer and grate it over the egg whites.

Bake for 15 to 20 minutes in the preheated oven, or until the surface is golden and baked through.

If you can't get hold of vanilla sugar, it's easy to make and keep in your pantry. Just take two vanilla beans and use a knife to split them down the middle. Cut them into 1¼-inch pieces and fill a small empty spice jar with sugar and vanilla. I would wait a week to allow the vanilla to infuse into the sugar. When you are ready to use the sugar, dispose of the vanilla pods.

This is such a delicious dessert that even though your guests may be full, I'm sure they will still indulge in a bissel of strudel pie.

jaffa chocolate mousse

serves 6

8 oz bittersweet or semi-sweet chocolate (the higher the percentage of cocoa solids, the bettter)

8 medium eggs, separated

3–4 tablespoons Cointreau

for decoration
grated orange-flavored dark chocolate

Whisk the egg whites until they form stiff peaks.

Melt the chocolate in a double boiler (bain-marie) on the stove-top over a gentle heat. If you don't have a double boiler, use a small bowl placed over a pan of hot water.

When the chocolate has melted, remove it from the heat.

Stir in the egg yolks one at a time.

Using a metal spoon, gently fold in one tablespoon of egg whites, then fold in the rest.

Add the Cointreau and stir gently.

Refrigerate.

Before serving, decorate the mousse with grated orange-flavored dark chocolate, if available.

lockshen pudding (noodle pudding)

serves 6

½ lb fine egg vermicelli, boiled
  and rinsed with cold water
1⅓ cups sultanas (golden
  or white raisins)
2 large eggs
2 teaspoons cinnamon
1 cooking apple, grated and
  drizzled with lemon juice
2 tablespoons sugar

1½ teaspoons almond extract
¼ cup non-dairy
  margarine, melted
2 tablespoons orange cordial

for topping
2 tablespoons sugar
1 teaspoon cinnamon

Preheat the oven to 375°F.

Mix all the ingredients, except the sugar and cinnamon for topping, and put the mixture into a greased ovenproof dish.

For the topping, mix the sugar together with the cinnamon and sprinkle over the pudding.

Bake in the preheated oven for 45 minutes to one hour.

The Friday night finale.

10

useful information

the jewish princess does yiddish

YID DISH? No, it's not a main course.

YID DISH? No, it's not a good-looking Jewish guy!

YIDD-ISH? No, it's not someone who is only a little bit Jewish.

YID D.I. SH? No, it's not a Jewish drill instructor!

yiddish is a wonderful language

The Yiddish language is like a recipe: take some German and add to it your Hebrew, season with Slavic, a teaspoon of Romanian, and finally, add a little English and French for that *je ne sais quoi*.

When used, you can express yourself in words that the listener doesn't have to understand to know exactly what you mean. The words have a warmth and earthiness to them. They are also incredibly powerful, as one word will convey feelings that you could not begin to sum up in paragraphs.

Remember *ch* is pronounced as if you are trying to clear your throat. *T* at the beginning of a word is silent; for example: *tsures* ("troubles") is pronounced *sur–es*.

In the following pages I have listed some of my favorite Yiddish words and expressions, many of which you will find within this book—and many of which, if you are a Jewish Princess, I am sure you already use.

Please note: because Yiddish comes originally from the Hebrew, and thus (like Greek) from no English-letter-based alphabet, English spellings vary from dictionary to dictionary, and even from person to person. Many Princesses have their own way of spelling, depending on where they were brought up. Spelling issues aside, I hope you find this useful when you are looking for just the right word to express how you feel!

yiddish/english glossary

Alter kocker An old person who looks old (obviously). Can't be found in Beverly Hills.
Ashkenazi A Jewish person from central or Eastern Europe.

Bagel Roll with a hole in the middle, eaten a lot on Sundays.
Balabatish An excellent homemaker. A true Jewish Princess!
Bar mitzvah A ceremony marking the religious coming of age of a 13-year-old boy (very expensive party).
Bashayrt Fate.
Bat mitzvah Ceremony marking the religious coming of age of a 12-year-old girl (also very expensive!).
Bissel A very small amount.
Blintz Pancake filled with cream cheese (*see* page 132).
Borscht Beet soup (*see* page 63).
Borscht Belt Popular holiday resort in the Catskill Mountains in upper New York State. For the European version, go to Grand Rimini in Italy.
Boychik Young boy.
Bris Circumcision for baby boys (ouch!).
Brocheh Blessing. There is a different one for every situation.
Broyges An argument with bad feeling. Happens a lot with families.
Bubbeleh Term of endearment—or a Passover pancake.
Bubbeh Grandmother (always imagine an old-looking grandma—not a

surgically enhanced Silver Surfer!).
Bubbeh-myseh Made-up story. I know some people—and they are all under 12—who are very good at these!
Bupkes Nothing.

Challah Plaited loaf used mainly for the Sabbath meal, delicious (*see* page 134 for Choca-Challah Pudding).
Challish To want something, as in "I *challish* for it."
Chanukah (or *Hanukkah*) The Festival of Lights (normally falls near Christmas). Eight days of presents: a JP's favorite time of the year!
Chasid Member of an orthodox religious sect.
Chayshik (pronounced *hay—shik*) Enthusiasm.
Chazzen Singer in Synagogue (like Neil Diamond in *The Jazz Singer* if you're lucky).
Chazzer Being greedy.
Cheder A school where children learn about the Jewish religion.
Chochem A clever person.
Cholent Meat stew that is cooked overnight (*see* page 96).
Chotchkeh Knickknack.
Chrayn Horseradish sauce. Delicious hot, red sauce that accompanies fish.
Chuppah Wedding canopy.
Chutzpah Audacity or nerve. A Jewish Princess has plenty of this!

Diaspora The historical dispersion of the Jews.
Doven Pray.
Drek A vulgar expression for ugly.

Farfel Tiny noodles.
Faygeleh Homosexual.
Feh! Ugh! Used when you don't like something.
Ferbissener A bitter person.
Fershtinkiner Revolting and smelly.
Flayshedik Kosher meat dishes.
Fliegel Chicken wing.
Forspeise A taster or appetizer.
Fress Eat a lot.
Frum Religious person.
Frummer Religious person.

Gatkes Long johns.
Gedempte Slowly cooked.
Gefilte fish A dish made from chopped fish; it can be fried or boiled.
Gelt Money.
Gesundheit You say it when someone sneezes and it means health.
Get A Jewish divorce.
Gavalt Shock. People usually say *Oy gavalt!* if something really bad happens.
Glatt kosher Strictly kosher.
Glitch When something goes wrong.
Golem Artificially created man.
Gonif A thief.
Gornisht Nothing.

Haggadah A book telling the Passover story.
Haimish (No, not a Scotsman...) Friendly and warm.
Halachah Religious law.

Halva Sweet confection made from sesame seeds (*see* page 138 for Honey Halva Ice Cream).
Hatikvah Israeli national anthem.

Kaddish Mourner's prayer.
Kapel or *Kippot* Skullcap Jewish men wear in synagogue—and, if religious, they wear all the time.
Kashrus Dietary laws.
Kibbutz Israeli cooperative agricultural settlement.
Kichel A cookie.
Kiddush Blessing recited over wine or bread on the Sabbath or at a festival.
Kinder Children.
Kishkes Guts.
Klutz Clumsy person.
Knaidlach Matzo balls (*see* page 196).
Knish Baked roll filled with potato or meat.
K'nocker A big shot. Or a big diamond.
Krank Something annoying.
Kreplach Ravioli with chopped meat.
Kugel Noodle or potato pudding.
Kvell To glow with pride.
Kvetch To complain.

Langer Lockshen Tall person, very thin—spaghetti-like.
Latke Potato pancake.
Lechayim (Lechaim) A toast to life.
Levoyah Funeral.
Loch in kop A hole in the head.
Lockshen Noodles.
Lox Smoked salmon.
Lubavitch A religious sect of orthodox Jews.

Macher An organizer.
Machetunim Relatives by marriage.
Matzo Unleavened bread.
Matzo-brie Matzo mixed with egg to make an omelette.
Mazel Good luck.
Mazel tov Congratulations.
Megillah A long story. It derives from the story of Esther at Purim.
Menorah Candelabra lit at Chanukah.
Mentsh A good person.
Meshugga Crazy, insane.
Meshuggener A crazy person.
Metsiah A bargain—like getting a Gucci handbag at 70 percent off!
Mezuzah Religious scroll in an encasement attached to a door.
Mieskayt An ugly person.
Mikvah A ritual bath.
Milchik Dairy foods.
Minyan Ten men required for religious services.
Mishegass A crazy idea.
Mitzvah A good idea.
Mockers Put bad luck on something.
Mogen Dovid A Star of David.
Mohel The man who performs the circumcision (ouch!).
Momzer Bastard.

Naches Pride from your children (*Shlepping naches* from the *kinder*).
Nebbish Nerdy person.
Noodge To nudge/remind.
Nosh Snacking: something I love to do!
Noo So?
Nudnik An annoying person.

Over shalom Passed away.

Oy! An exclamation of surprise.
Oy veh! An exclamation of shock.

Parev Foods that contain no dairy products.
Pesach Passover.
Pish To urinate.
Pletzel Like a bagel without the hole and with poppy seeds and onion on top.
Polkeh Chicken drumstick.
Puppik Navel.
Putz Idiot.

Rachmones Pity.
Rebbe Rabbi.
Rebbitsen Rabbi's wife.
Rosh Hashana The Jewish New Year.

Saychel Common sense; using your head.
Seder The meal we eat first and second night of Passover.
Sefer Torah The scroll containing the five Books of Moses.
Sephadi A Jewish person from Spanish or Portuguese descent.
Shabbos The Sabbath.
Shadchen A matchmaker.
Shah Shut up!
Sha'koyach Congratulations.
Shalom (Sholom) Peace.
Shamus No, not an Irish person— a detective.
Shayn Pretty.
Sheitel A wig worn by a married Orthodox woman.
Shiddach A possible marriage introduction.
Shiker Drunk.

Shissel A cooking pot.

Shivah A seven-day period of mourning.

Shlemiel An idiot.

Shlep To carry or to go a long way.

Shlepper Someone who carries all your heavy goods.

Shloch An untidy person.

Shlong The male organ (large).

Shluff To have a sleep.

Shmaltz Chicken fat. Or being too sentimental (no, I don't know why, either).

Shmatta Rags, cheap clothes. Can be said sarcastically when you are wearing your brand-new D&G.

Shmear To spread ("A *shmear* of cream cheese on my bagel, please.") Or to bribe.

Shmendrick An idiot.

Shmo An idiot.

Shmooze To coax with charming behavior (JPs are very good at this).

Shmuck An idiot. Or a penis...

Shmutzy Looking unkempt or dirty.

Shnide To do something underhanded.

Shnorrer A mean person.

Shochet The ritual slaughter of animals for kosher meat.

Shofar A ram's horn blown in synagogues on the new year.

Shpilkes When you are restless.

Shpritz A spray or squirt of something.

Shtetl Jewish village in Eastern Europe.

Shtick Something that is funny.

Shtook In trouble.

Shtoom! Keep quiet! Can be said to children when noisy or when you want to keep something quiet.

Shtup A vulgar word for sexual intercourse; it also means tipped.

Shul Synagogue

Shvitz To be hot.

Shyster A thief or unscrupulous person.

Siddur A prayer book.

Simcha A joyous occasion. A common expression is "Only on *simchas*."

Smetana A type of sour cream.

Spiel A salesman's patter when he's talking to a client.

Tallis A Jewish prayer shawl (not a pashmina...).

Talmud Jewish law and tradition.

Tush Backside.

Torah The Five Books of Moses.

Treif See page 18. Un-kosher—shrimp, pork, etc.

Tsedrayt A crazy person.

Tsures Troubles.

Tzaddik A righteous man.

Tzimmes (*see* page 98) A dish of cooked meat and vegetables, sometimes with added fruit.

Worsht (pronounced *vorsht*) Salami.

Yachna A gossip.

Yahrtzeit The anniversary of a death.

Yamulka Skullcap—same as *kapel*.

Yenta A female gossip.

Yiches Prestige.

Yiddishe Jewish.

Yiddishkeit Jewishness.

Yom kippur The Day of Atonement.

Yom tov A Jewish holiday.

Zaydeh Grandfather.

Zey gezunt Go in good health.

princess pointers

Every Princess knows that a little bit of advice can be invaluable (except when it comes from your mother-in-law). In the kitchen, having a few tips up your sleeve not only makes life easier, but it can also cut down on time, stop your hands smelling of onions, and—most importantly— impress your mother-in-law. So here are a few that I find most handy.

1   If you place some paper towels folded double on top of your chicken soup, then lift it off, all the fat comes away with it.

2   If you're looking for *challah*, matzo meal, chicken-soup mix, dairy-free creamer or dairy-free margarine, just try your local kosher deli or the kosher section at your supermarket.

3   When cutting fresh bread and cake, first dip your knife in boiling water. You will get a beautifully clean slice.

4   A glass will not crack or break if you place a spoon in it first before pouring in hot liquid (Science Teacher, a.k.a. son aged 12, taught me that one).

5   When presenting food or arranging your flowers, always use odd numbers.

6   Prick sausages with a fork before cooking, because this prevents them from bursting.

7   When slicing an onion, don your rubber gloves to avoid smelly hands. Let the water run to avoid sliding mascara—or better still, buy frozen, ready-sliced onions.

8   If your soup or stew is too salty, add a teaspoon of sugar or a little grated raw potato and cook gently for a few minutes.

9   When chopping herbs, use a pair of kitchen scissors.

10   When peeling hard-boiled eggs, immerse them in cold water, then roll on paper towels to remove the shells.

11   If a guest offers to bring a dish, say "YES!"

12   Always check your pantry for ingredients before baking.

13   Always, always turn the oven on *before* you start making a cake, so that it will reach the correct temperature.

14   Double up! If you're going to the trouble of making a cake, why not make two and freeze one? Then you're always prepared for those surprise guests.

15   Get the kids involved. This has many benefits. Firstly, it turns them on to cooking (future Princes and Princesses). Secondly, it makes them more adventurous when it comes to eating. Thirdly, they will be able to cook for you in your old age.

16   If you have great help, hang on to her (or even *him*). Don't forget to offer praise for doing a great job.

17   Always wash your hands before cooking, and after you have handled raw meat and eggs.

18   When using eggs, always crack them into a glass bowl, one at a time, before adding them to any other ingredients. This helps avoid any shell fragments falling into the mixture, and you can also see if any are bad (or unkosher, if they contain blood spots).

19   Insert a sharp blade into a cake to see if it's done. If it comes out clean, your cake has baked.

20 To get a cake out of the pan easily, make sure you grease (with butter) and flour it before pouring in the mixture—regardless of whether or not the recipe calls for it.

21 When removing a cake from a loose-bottomed pan, place the pan on a tin can and press down to lift off the sides.

22 Don't forget to use confectioners sugar—it's like fairy dust. Sprinkle over cakes and fruit for that little extra touch.

23 When using a loose-bottomed pan, wrap aluminum foil around the bottom to prevent the mixture from seeping out. This prevents your oven from getting dirty.

24 When you are at the checkout, don't be afraid to ask for a packer—or better still, shop online.

25 Check your sell-by dates. After all, you won't want to poison your family—so if in doubt, throw it out.

26 Know your oven like a friend. They all vary, and some cook quicker than others, so keep this in mind when following recipes.

27 Don't forget: if you spend a long time in the car (and most JPs do this) always have water, tissues, coins for parking meters, Junior JP snacks, hand cream, and Tylenol on hand.

28 When buying aluminum foil, parchment paper, and plastic wrap, always buy the jumbo size.

29 Wear your Jewish Princess apron when cooking to protect those *couture* creations.

30 Always wear your Jewish Princess oven gloves to protect your perfect manicure.

the jewish princess parting note

The Jewish Princess loves to party, but you don't need to go to a party in order to *parteee!* Every day can be a party. It's just how you decide to live your life.

Find your inner Princess and you will see that the little things in life—like eating with your friends and family, sitting down and having a nice cup of tea, laughing on the phone at some amusing tale, or treating yourself to a little something (I find handbags always cheer me up enormously) . . . in other words, finding the things that make you happy (and often this means *making others* happy)—will show you that the Jewish Princess Champagne Theory is true.

"What's the Jewish Princess Champagne Theory?" I hear you ask.

Well, here it is:

"Is the Champagne Bottle of Life half-full or half-empty?"

For every Jewish Princess, the answer is: "The Champagne Bottle of Life is ALWAYS half-full."

But of course, she always orders another bottle to keep in reserve. (She can't help it. It's genetic.)

I know that the pace of this hectic world can sometimes make you feel like you're riding on a very fast train and hanging on for dear life; well, hang on in there, because eventually you *will* get to your destination. If you just try and arrive in style, however, no one will ever be the wiser.

Anyway, enough of Princess Philosophy.

What I really want to say is GOODBYE until the next time we meet, which I am sure will be very soon, since we live in a very small world. Of course, being a Jewish Princess I hate to say goodbye; I prefer to say *shalom*.

Peace to all my Princess People, whether you are Jewish, Christian, Catholic, Hindu, Muslim, Atheist . . . Let's try and find our common ground, so that we can come together and share our cultures and our recipes.

Let us sit down for dinner sometime and enjoy the simple things in life (like Bvlgari jewelry).

Now I really must go—I have a very important meeting. Yes, you guessed it: HAIRDRESSER!

I may be gone for a while, since I need my color done, so while I'm away, just remember the Three Ps:

* positive
* productive

And, of course:
* princesslike!

XXXXXXXXXXX

if all else fails…

…call the caterer!